Recipes from the Hearth

At home with South African icons
FOOD **FRANCOIS FERREIRA** *WITH* **GWYNNE CONLYN**

First published by Gwynne Conlyn Publishing in 2007

In association with Jacana Media

10 Orange Street, Sunnyside
Auckland Park 2092, South Africa
+2711 628 3200
www.jacana.co.za
www.gwynneconlyn.com

© Photographs, recipes and text: Annelie Rabie, Business Against Crime Western Cape;
Design: Jacana Media in association with Gwynne Conlyn Publishing

All rights reserved.
ISBN 978-0-620-39512-0

Cover design by Jacana Media
Set in Sabon
Photography: Brandon Amron Coetzee
Styling: Kanyacilla Hunt
Production assistants:
From Bergzicht Training Centre, Stellenbosch: Kristin Dillen,
Celeste Fernandez, Maria Booysen, Muriel Abrahams
From PGW Eat: ICA student Harold van Rooyen
From Business Against Crime Western Cape: Jackie Archer

Printed by CTP Book Printers
Job No. 000533

See a complete list of titles at www.jacana.co.za and www.gwynneconlyn.com

Contents

Foreword by Mary van Apeldoorn 2
Cass Abrahams 4
  Smoorsnoek Bundles 6
Raymond Ackerman 10
  Apple and Berry Tart. 12
Allan Barnard 16
  Greek-Style Calamari Pan Stew 18
Sheila Camerer. 22
  Oven-baked Yellowtail 24
Yvonne Chaka Chaka 28
  Chicken and Mushroom Casserole . . 30
Renata Coetzee 34
  Rooibos Smoked Ostrich
  Carpaccio served with a
  Sorrel-Buttermilk Sauce. 36
Annette Cowley Nel. 40
  Chuchi Goong
  (King Prawns in Red Curry) 42
FW and Elita de Klerk 46
  Lakhano Dolmades
  (Stuffed Cabbage Leaves). 48
Denise Dogon 52
  Chicken with Herb & Lemon
  Marinade and Grilled Vegetables. . . . 54

Lillian Dube. 58
  Lillian's Sardines 60
Billy Gallagher. 64
  Pumpkin and Biltong Soup. 66
Gwen Gill. 70
  My Mum's Trashy but Terrific Trifle . . 72
Pam Golding 76
  Pam Golding's Favourite
  Fish Soufflé 78
Dr Patricia Gorvalla. 82
  Malva Pudding 84
Anthony and Olive Hamilton Russell. . 88
  Fig and Pistachio Tart 90
Susan Huxter and Margot Janse. 94
  Choc-chip and Nut Brownies 96
Vaughan Johnson. 100
  Bobotie 102
Basetsana Kumalo 106
  Peri Peri Prawns 108
Reg Lascaris 112
  Fillet in Pastry 114
Vanya Mangaliso 118
  Tropical Fruit Kebabs 120

Dr Ivan R May 124
  Ouma's Granadilla Pudding 126

Ina Paarman 130
  Butter Bean and Roast
  Vegetable Salad 132

Aviva Pelham 136
  Warm Fluffy Baked Cheesecake. . . . 138

Francois Pienaar. 142
  Grilled Herb-marinated Portabella
  Mushrooms with Gorgonzola. 144

Gary Player 148
  Pear and Goat's Cheese
  with Rocket and Lemon Oil 150

Gavin Rajah 154
  The Raj's Decadent
  Chocolate Cake. 156

Jane Raphaely 160
  Whole Roasted Chinese Fish 162

Lannice Snyman. 166
  Chicken with Peaches and
  Pancetta on Mashed Cauliflower. . . 168

Peter Soldatos 172
  Rice Pudding. 174

Beyers Truter 178
  Jumbo Pinotage Lamb Burger 180

Desmond Tutu. 184
  Tutu Chicken 186

Walter Ulz 190
  Salmon Carpaccio topped
  with Seafood Cerviche. 192

Mary van Apeldoorn 196
  Fish Cakes. 199

Peter Veldsman 202
  Beef and Pork 'Pie' 204

Topsi Venter 208
  Polenta Terrine with Chevre and
  Pickled Red and Yellow Peppers . . . 210

Martin Welz 214
  Slow-cooked Oxtail and Beans 216

Foreword

What you are holding is not just another cookbook! It is a dedication to the many men and women who on a daily basis make a significant contribution to the wonderful land we call South Africa. Whilst this book was conceptualised by Business Against Crime Western Cape, it soon grew into a project celebrating the life, commitment and enthusiasm of a number of icons covering all aspects of life.

Sincere appreciation is expressed towards the icons who generously donated their recipes and life's tales to be included in this book. All of these participants in one way or another play a major role in shaping the future of South Africa in all walks of life: arts, culture, couture, property, food and wine, music, politics, entertaining, media, business.

The proceeds of this book will be used to contribute towards the projects facilitated by Business Against Crime Western Cape. Business Against Crime Western Cape is a project management organisation which partners Government in the strategic fight against crime. Whilst crime generally conjures up feelings of negativity and despair, the results of projects of this organisation certainly indicate that there are untold numbers of people and organisations both public and private that assist in dealing with the scourge. This book also pays tribute to the excellent working relationship between Business Against Crime Western Cape and the South African Police Service, Western Cape lead by a very capable and business-minded Mzwandile Petros.

Business Against Crime Western Cape is hugely indebted to Chef Francois Ferreira who donated his time, energy and love for cooking and testing each recipe; the vivacious Gwynne Conlyn who used her publishing creativity and commitment to the fight against crime to produce this wonderful tribute; Brandon Amron Coetzee a highly talented photographer; and Kanyacilla Hunt, a stylist par excellence. Jackie Archer of Business Against Crime Western Cape deserves a very special word of thanks for her dedication and perseverance for keeping the paper chain in place and on target!

Enjoy the wonderful personal recipes and heart delights of the icons! Every time this book is used, you should remind yourself of the contribution you have graciously made towards the strategic fight against crime.

Mary van Apeldoorn
Non-executive Director and project sponsor
Business Against Crime Western Cape
Cape Town

31 August 2007

Dedicated to the spirit of the people that embody South Africa.

Cass Abrahams

Malay 'Culinary and Cultural Activist'

Cass Abrahams might have carved a niche for herself as a Malay cookery expert, but it is really her reputation as a culinary and cultural activist that makes her feel alive.

Says Cass, "I married into the Cape Malay community and made it one of my life's projects to research my husband's family – where they came from, for instance, the origins of their colloquial expressions, their culinary traditions."

This fascinating journey has also taken Cass to the stage with her daughter, Rehana. They enthralled audiences at the Grahamstown National Arts Festival with their show, *Spice Root*. On stage Cass told stories of the spice routes of the 17th Century – through cooking. "Imagine," says Cass, "the history of the Malay people told through the aromas and even the tastes of food!"

"What is fascinating," says this remarkable woman, "is the way history is reflected in our food. Wars, joys, laughter – even geography, weather conditions and therefore available ingredients – it's all tied up in a plate of food".

Cass is also a chef, as well as the author of two cookbooks.

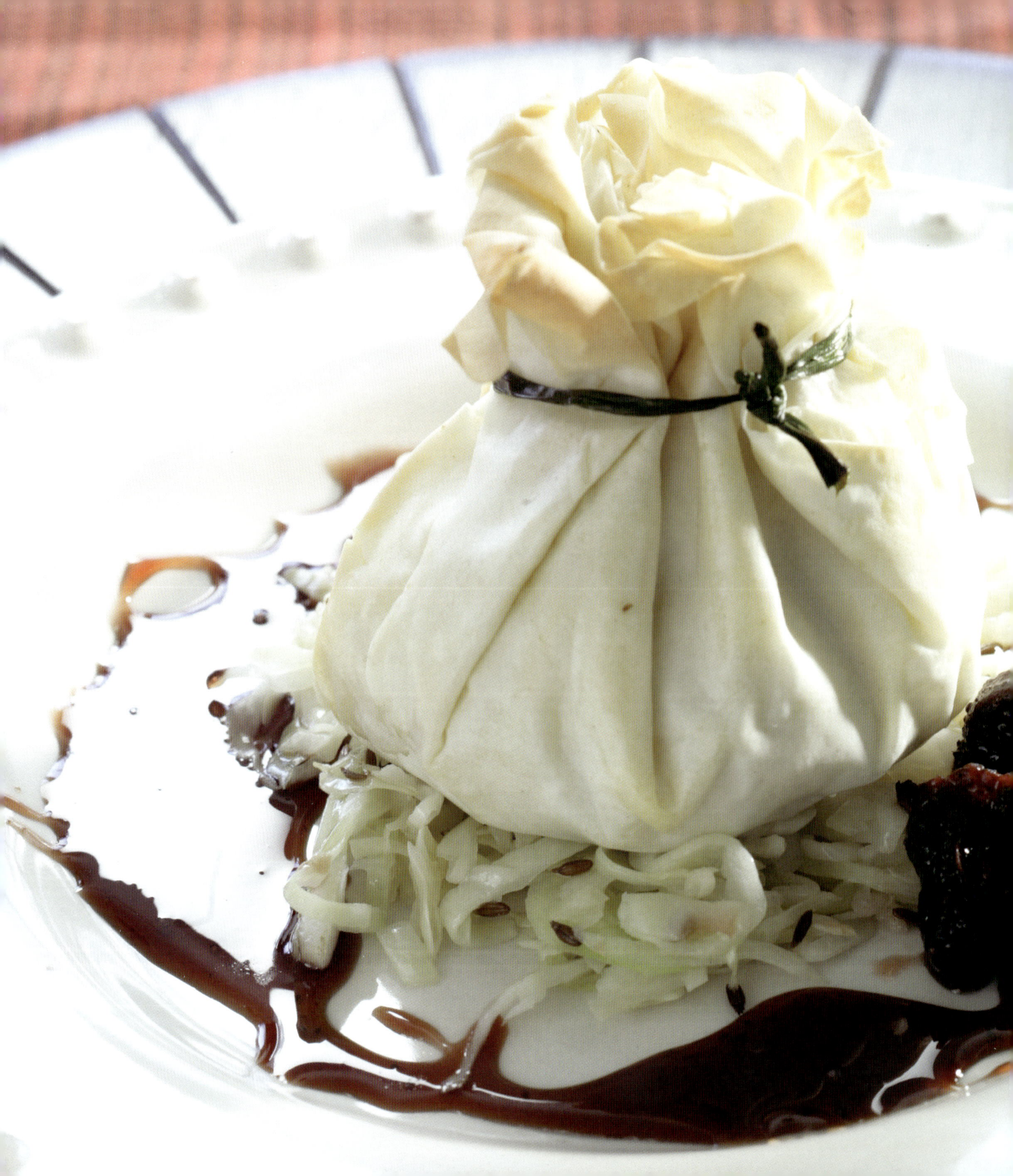

Smoorsnoek Bundles

Smoorsnoek is one of the oldest recipes in South Africa – it is usually made with salted and air-dried snoek mixed with tomato, onion, spices and potatoes.

Ingredients

Mouth-watering smoorsnoek in phyllo pastry is best served on toasted cumin cabbage with a sour fig and balsamic sauce.

100g	butter, melted
	cooked smoorsnoek
	phyllo pastry

Toasted Cumin Cabbage

10ml	oil
10ml	cumin seeds
	½ cabbage, shredded

Sour Fig and Balsamic Sauce

125ml	sour figs preserve
	balsamic vinegar to taste

Serves 6

Method

Smoorsnoek is made by flaking either fresh cooked snoek, smoked snoek or, as tradition dictates, salted snoek; and cooking it with a concasse of tomato and onion, potato with a touch of ginger, garlic and a hint of chilli.

Place one sheet of phyllo on working surface (cover sheets you are not using with a damp cloth). Cut into 4 equal squares of about 25cm each. Brush each square with melted butter and place on top of each other to form a 16-point star.

Place 1 tablespoon smoorsnoek in the centre of the pastry and gather up the edges to form a parcel. Tie loosely with string and fluff up the pastry edges.

Brush parcel with butter. Place on a greased baking tray. Repeat until you've made enough for your requirements.

Bake at 180°C until golden brown.

Toasted Cumin Cabbage

Heat oil in a pan; add the cumin seeds and fry until brown.

Add the cabbage and stir-fry for 3 minutes over high heat.

Sour Fig and Balsamic Sauce

Mix enough balsamic vinegar into the sour figs to achieve a pleasant sweet-sour taste.

Notes

To assemble: place about two tablespoons of cabbage on a plate. Place the snoek parcel on top and drizzle the sauce around the parcel.

Raymond Ackerman

Founder, Pick 'n Pay

Raymond Ackerman and his company Pick 'n Pay, the country's most successful retail supermarket chain, are as South African as braaivleis and rugby. But it is his spirit of 'ubuntu' – and he has a string of awards bearing testament to his inherent caring for his fellow South Africans – that is almost certainly the bedrock on which his phenomenal success was built.

When Ackerman took a bank loan back in 1966 to buy four small Cape Town supermarkets, it's unlikely that anyone realised he'd be such a safe bet. Only a year later, the stores did a turnover of R3 million – no small achievement for any new businessman.

But today the Pick 'n Pay Group, of which Ackerman is chairman, comprises 513 supermarkets and hypermarkets, as well as 191 franchised outlets, employing over 50 000 people and notching up an annual turnover around R40 billion.

The father of four was the only South African to be rated amongst the World's Top 100 Leaders in 2004, but there's no doubt he'll say that his biggest success is being in a position to help change the lives of others who need a hand up.

His vision has turned to a reality most can only dream of, but Ackerman remains adamant that everything his company does is underpinned by a caring, concerned attitude to others, and a desire to uplift those who are less fortunate.

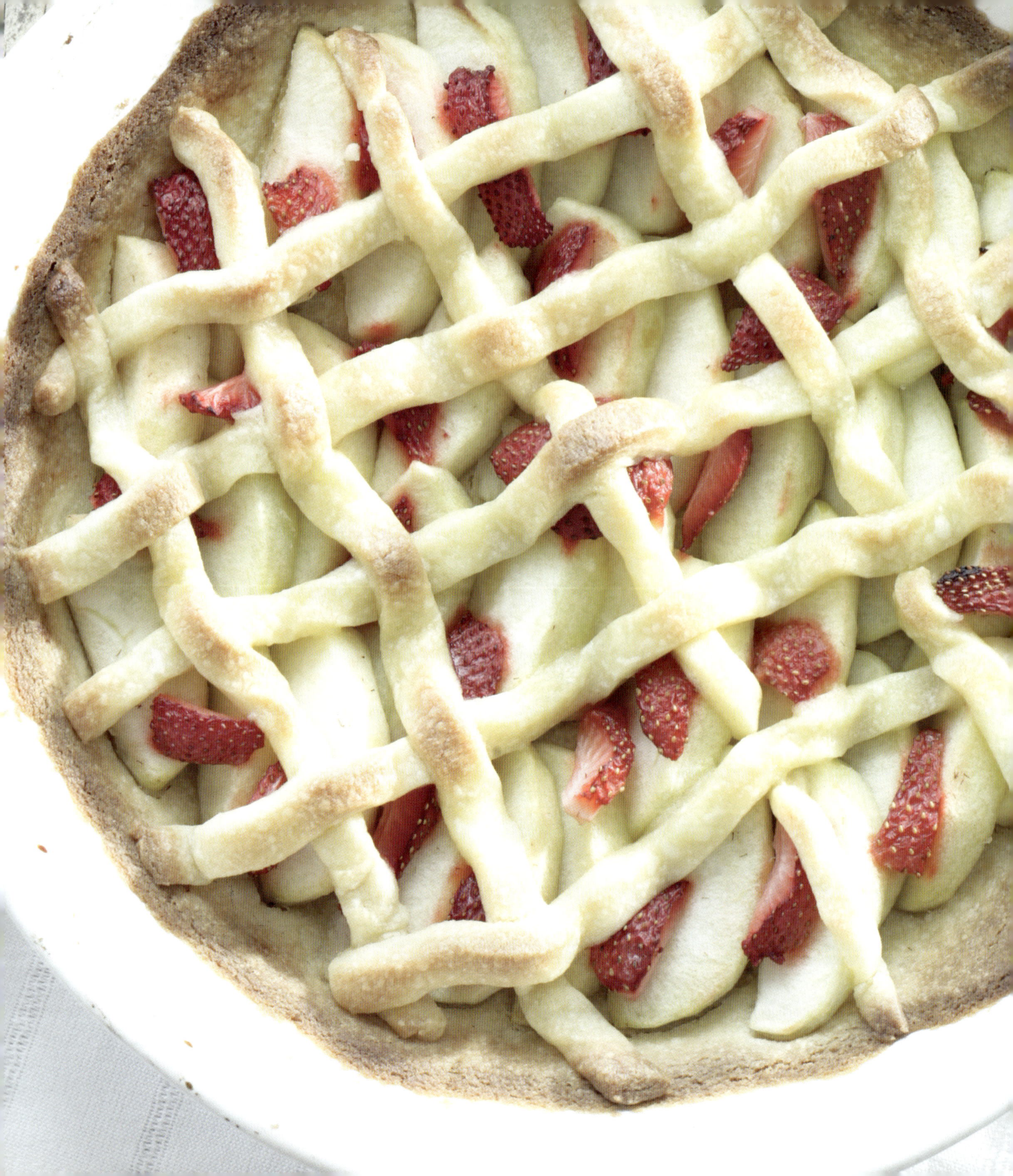

Apple and Berry Tart

This has become a family favourite in our household. It's delicious warm with custard, or cold with cream, and I do hope you will enjoy it as much as I do!

Ingredients

Pastry

125g	margarine
80ml	castor sugar
500ml	flour
5ml	baking powder
1	egg

Filling

6	large granny smith apples, peeled and sliced
30ml	lemon rind
60ml	sugar
60ml	water
250ml	strawberries cut in half
375ml	fresh or frozen berries
17ml	water
30ml	sugar

Serves 6

Method

Pastry

Beat margarine and castor sugar until light and fluffy.

Add egg and stir in the flour and baking powder to make a firm dough.

Roll into 2 x 24cm circles and refrigerate for 30 minutes, or until firm

Filling

Preheat the oven to 180°C.

Simmer the apples for 10 minutes with the lemon rind, sugar and water. Set aside to cool.

Press one pastry circle into bottom of a spring form tin or into an ovenproof quiche dish.

Spread apples, strawberries and berries on top.

Cut remaining dough into strips and place in a crisscross pattern on top of fruit. Brush with water and sprinkle with sugar.

Bake for roughly 15-20 minutes until pastry is cooked and brown.

Serve with custard or cream.

Allan Barnard

567 Cape Talk *Radio Presenter*

Someone once told Allan Barnard he had "a nice voice for radio" – and a good thing that was too, considering his huge fan-base across the Western Cape. The *567 Cape Talk* mid-morning presenter on weekends earned his stripes over more than two decades, first at *Good Hope FM* and then at *94.5 Kfm*, but still jokes that his job is a far cry from his young hopes of becoming South Africa's president.

This is the man who loves listening to French ballads – "they just ooooze l-u-r-v-e" – but when it comes to what really soothes him, Barnard is far more practical: "Lying under an air conditioner in 42-degree heat in my village of Riebeek Kasteel!" But he does admit to a secret indulgence: buying an obscenely expensive can of real French Foie Gras at a local deli "and having it all to myself".

Born on the West Coast and raised in Cape Town, Barnard says his mother – "the most honest person I've ever known" – has been the greatest influence on his life. And, clearly, a good influence too, because this popular radio presenter, with the voice as smooth as thick golden syrup, admits he'd go to the ends of the earth for all his friends.

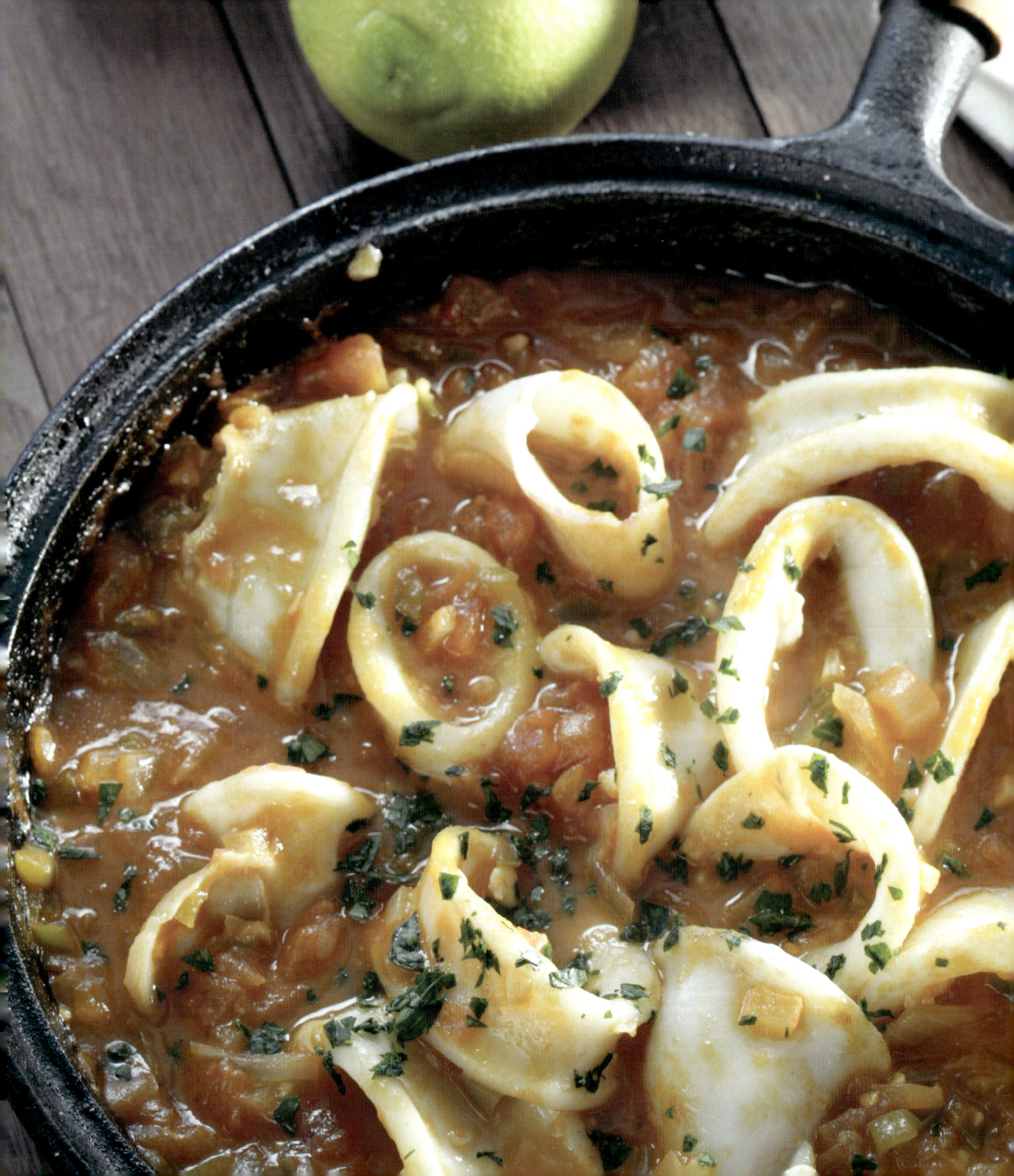

Greek-Style Calamari Pan Stew

This dish is ideal for a lazy summer afternoon. Serve with crusty bread, good olive oil and a gorgeous salad.

Ingredients

1kg	cleaned calamari tubes (cut into rings, if you like) – make sure they are patted dry before you cook them
6	large, very ripe tomatoes, peeled, seeded and roughly chopped
4	cloves garlic, chopped
125ml	lemon juice
1	medium onion, roughly chopped
5ml	finely chopped chilli (optional)
125ml	parsley, finely chopped
1	green pepper, finely chopped
15ml	butter
15ml	olive oil
	salt and crushed black pepper

Serves 4

Method

Heat half the oil and half the butter in a saucepan. Add the onion, garlic, green pepper and chilli and fry at medium heat for about 3 minutes until soft.

Add the tomatoes and lemon juice and let simmer for 10 minutes.

In a separate pan, heat the rest of the oil and butter and turn up the heat until the pan just starts to smoke (take care!).

At this point, add the calamari and cook 2-3 minutes.

Remove from heat and transfer all of the calamari to the simmering mixture.

Cook for a further 2 minutes, add the parsley at the last minute and serve.

Sheila Camerer

Democratic Alliance
Member of Parliament

Senior Member of Parliament, Sheila Camerer, was around in the bad old days when Parliament was a quintessential boys' club, and she was viewed as something of "a doll" by the male MPs who didn't take their few female colleagues very seriously. The difference is that Camerer is still there, and just shortly into South Africa's new democracy was speaking with genuine warmth about the camaraderie she had found in the parliamentary "sisterhood".

Today Camerer is one of three top women in the official opposition, the Democratic Alliance, as federal legal commission chairperson. She's outspoken on issues of justice and equity, especially for women, working tirelessly since becoming active in politics in 1982 when her children were grown up. By then this multi-talented woman had worked as a mother, lawyer, journalist and legal consultant, but the path to Parliament was cleared when she shocked many and joined the National Party, becoming a Johannesburg city councillor, and later NP MP for Rosettenville in 1987.

What's not widely known is that as a young lawyer in the mid-1970s, Camerer actually worked on the legal defence strategies of anti-apartheid activists, including that of the Soweto Committee of Ten. Camerer definitely prefers the new South Africa Parliament, describing it as livelier and more cheerful, and "much more caring about women's concerns". And one of her best experiences in politics? "Definitely in (Former President) Nelson Mandela's Cabinet as Deputy Minister of Justice", said Sheila.

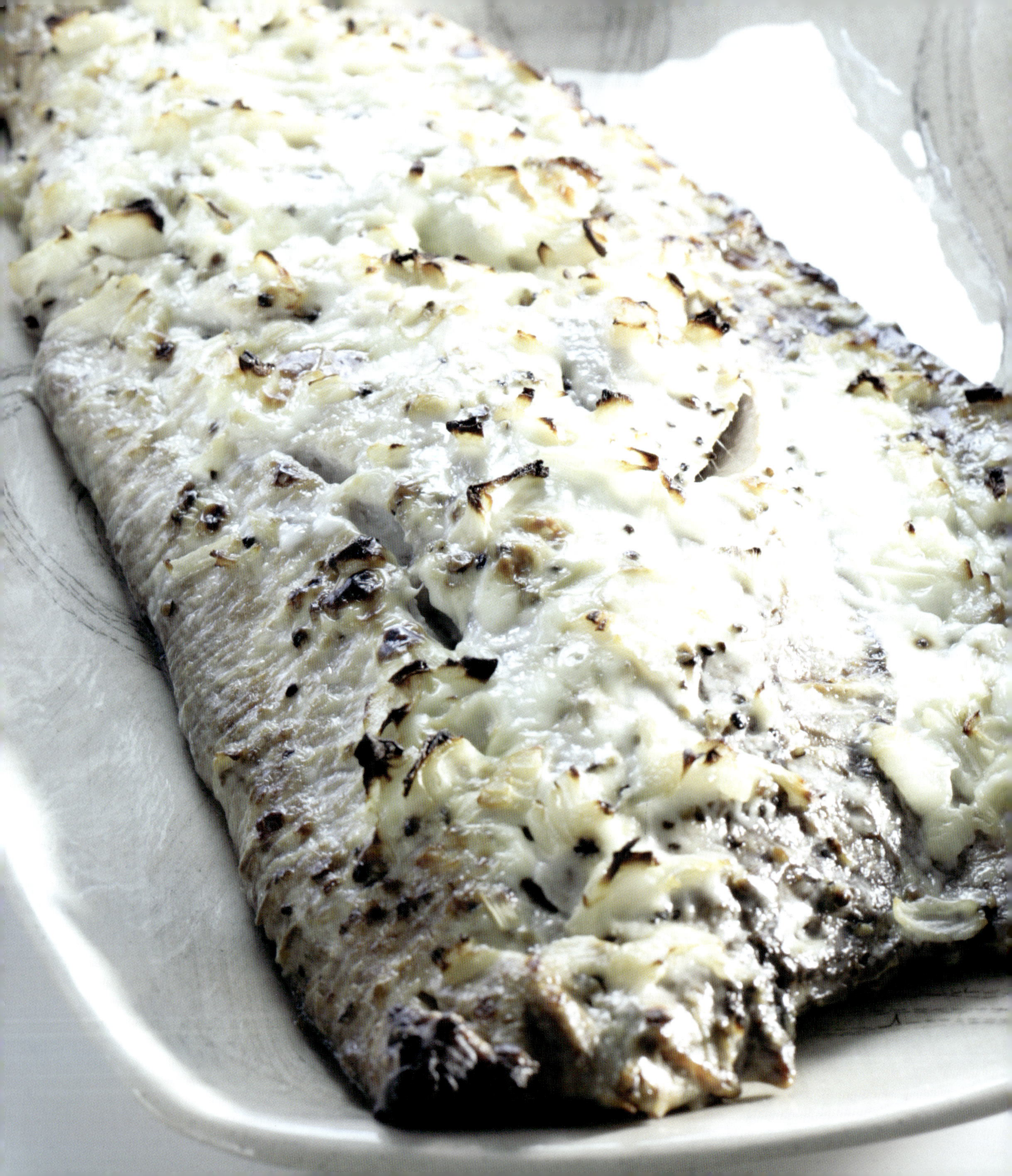

Oven-baked Yellowtail

I love to cook but seldom have time because of my work. If my favourite recipe will help a good cause, it's a win-win situation!

Ingredients

1	medium-sized yellowtail (about 1,2kg)
120ml	creamy mayonnaise
2	large onions finely chopped
	juice of 2 lemons
	salt and black pepper to taste

Serves 4-6

Method

Preheat oven to 180°C.

Open and spread out the yellowtail so that it lies flat in one piece on a baking dish. Retain the skin on the underside.

Sprinkle with lemon juice, salt and pepper.

Chop the onions very fine.

Spread mayonnaise thickly over the fish and sprinkle onions on top.

Bake for 45 minutes.

Serve with baby potatoes, baked in olive oil.

Notes

Garnish with sprigs of rosemary, peas and baked whole tomatoes.

Yvonne Chaka Chaka

Princess of Song

She's the "Princess of Africa", the entertainment icon with the powerful alto vocals who won the hearts of fans nationally and throughout Africa. From bubblegum pop star in the 1980s to talkshow presenter and host in the new millennium, Yvonne Chaka Chaka has been at the forefront of popular South African music for more than 20 years.

But ask anyone and they'll tell you that this is a star whose head has not been turned by her success – whether she's performing for kings and queens, presidents and first ladies or at corporate concerts, she always returns to her fans and family of listeners in South Africa's cities, townships and rural regions. She's rubbed shoulders with the likes of Nelson Mandela, Britain's Queen Elizabeth and world-renowned United States talkshow host Oprah Winfrey, but still she maintains her humility and takes it all in her stride.

Chaka Chaka first hit the South African music charts as a teenager in 1984 with the explosive hit "I'm in Love with a DJ", which sold 35 000 copies. But through it all, the person she most admires in the world is her mother who raised her and her two sisters single-handedly on a domestic worker's salary.

Chaka Chaka says she's blessed to have realised her destiny.

What's a certainty is that her popularity and accomplishments have already ensured her legacy as one of the greatest stars to light up the African continent.

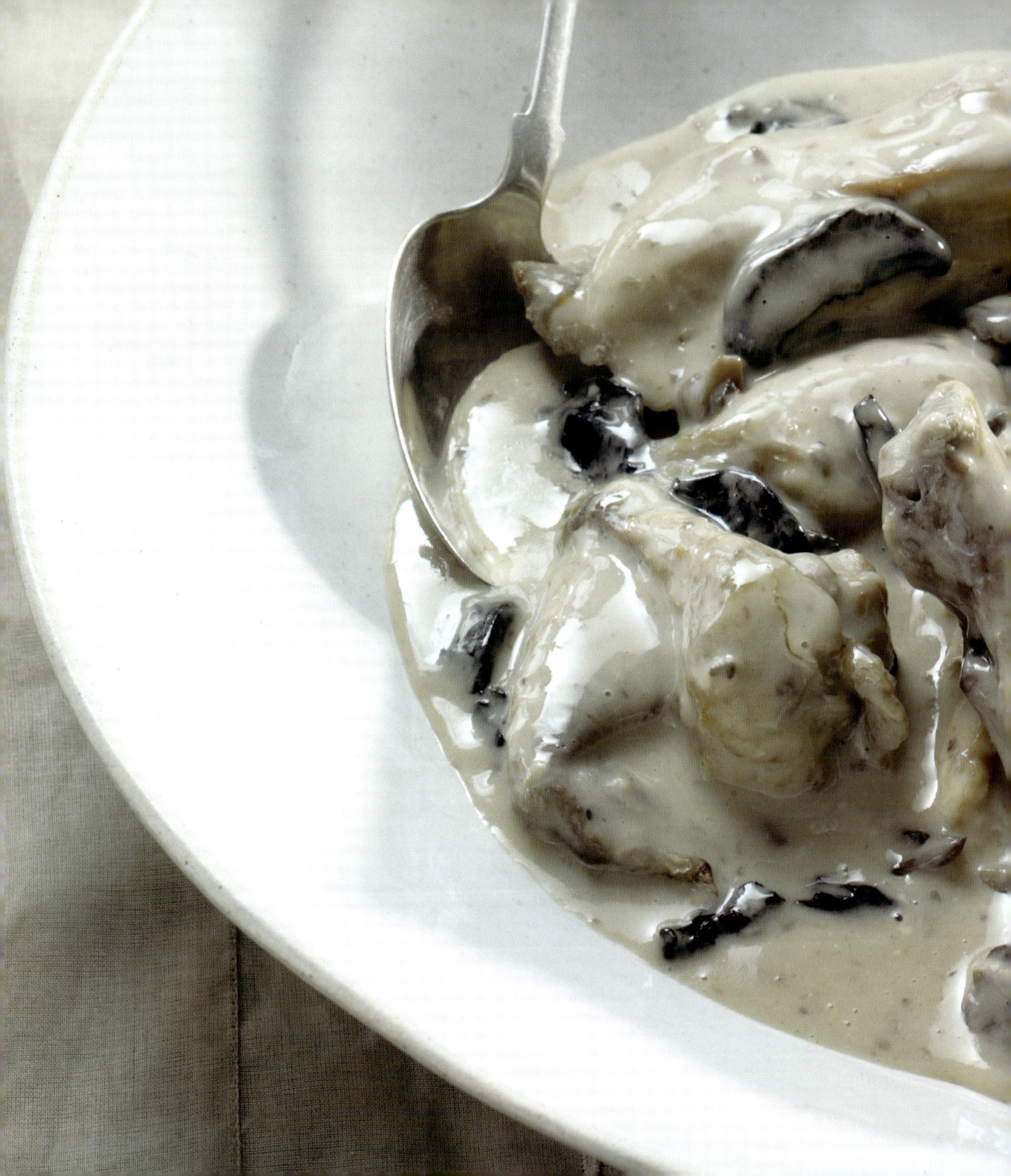

Chicken and Mushroom Casserole

To add some extra zing to this dish – try hydrating some shitake or porcini mushrooms and add it to the mixture.

Ingredients

1.5kg	chicken pieces
60g	butter
15ml	olive oil
470g	tin cream of chicken soup
500ml	water
125ml	cream
15ml	flour
250g	mushrooms, sliced
1ml	crushed dried rosemary
5ml	chopped parsley

Serves 4-6

Method

Preheat the oven to 180°C.

In a large saucepan, heat the butter and olive oil. Add the chicken pieces and gently cook until browned all over. Remove from the pan.

Drain half the fat in the pan off, then add the sliced mushrooms and sauté gently for about 3 minutes. Sprinkle the flour over the mushrooms and stir until well combined.

Remove the pan from the heat and add the tin of chicken soup and the water. Stir until all the ingredients have combined. Return the pan to the heat, bring to the boil, stirring continuously.

As the sauce thickens, add the cream, salt, pepper, rosemary and parsley. Put the chicken pieces into an ovenproof dish, and pour the sauce over the chicken.

Cover the ovenproof dish and place in the preheated oven and cook for one hour or until the chicken is tender.

Remove from the oven and serve with rice and vegetables.

Renata Coetzee

*Indigenous African Cuisine
Historian and Scientist*

Nobody knows that food and culture are inextricably linked more than indigenous African cuisine historian and scientist Renata Coetzee. Whether its samp, bean and meat stew, or souskluitjies and soetkoekies, Coetzee has meticulously recorded the diversity of South African eating habits from way back in 1652.

In fact, her work is so unique that the North West University conferred an honorary doctorate on Coetzee in recognition of her pioneering work in the field of indigenous food and traditional African cuisine. Want to know what the early Cape Dutch community was cooking up between 1652 and 1800? It's all in her classic *The South African Culinary Tradition*, published in 1977, in which she examines the relationships between cultural background, eating habits and social practices. Food habits, cultural practices and traditional behaviour were also the focus of another of her works, *Funa: Food from Africa*, but this time in respect of the country's indigenous people.

Coetzee is recognised for her valuable contribution to the commercialisation of indigenous foods in several development programmes, to help alleviate poverty and empower women in rural areas. And crowds of hungry people have never intimidated the multi-talented Coetzee either.

The former Potchefstroom campus student was section manager for dietetics and catering in Anglo-American's gold and uranium section, after which she worked as senior dietitian at Stellenbosch University, where her responsibilities included the preparation of food at 21 residences, 6 banquet halls and 2 student cafeterias.

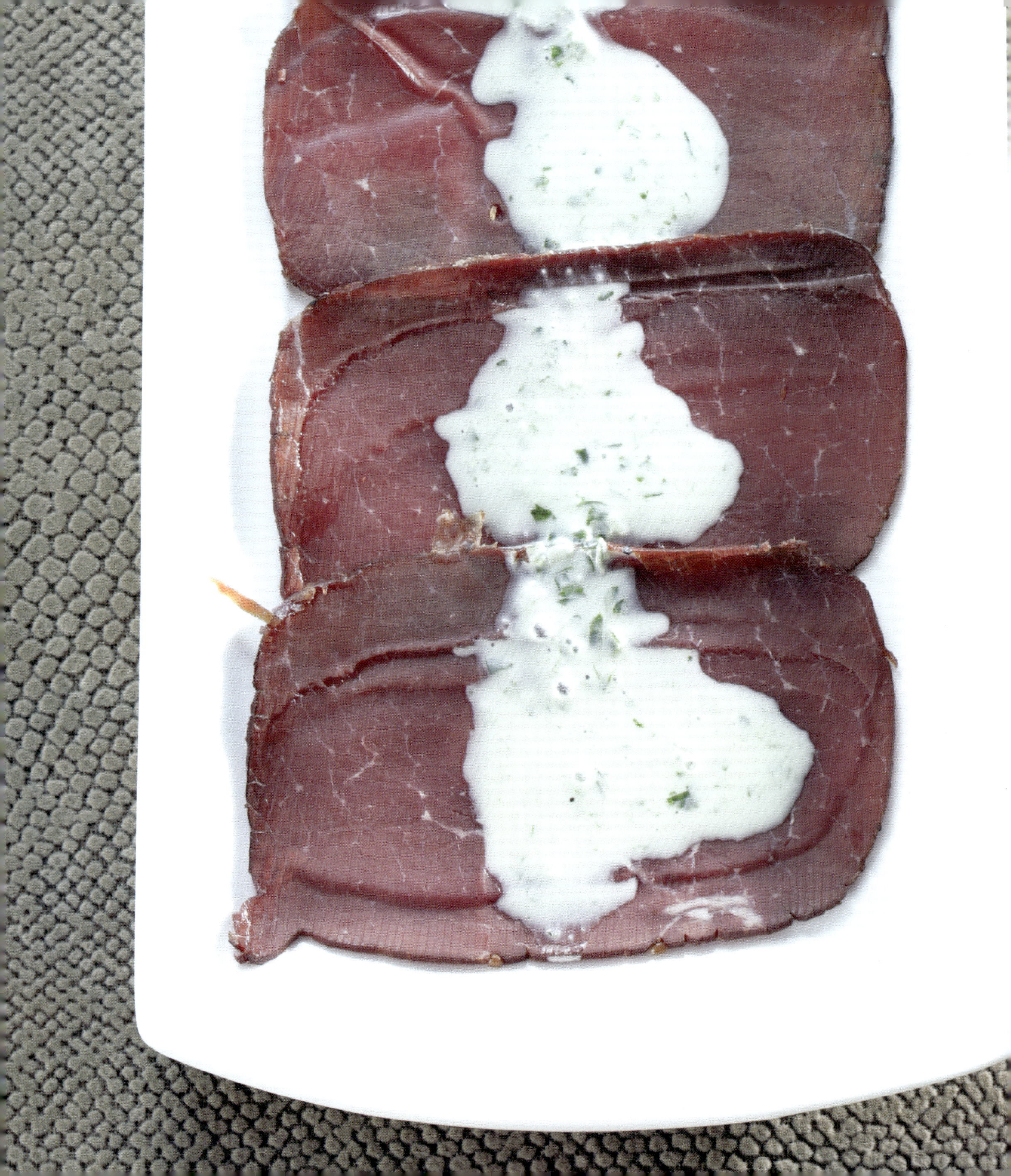

Rooibos Smoked Ostrich Carpaccio served with a Sorrel-Buttermilk Sauce

The Khoikhoi had been living in the Western Cape some 2 000 years before the European settlers and the African farmers arrived. The food of the Khoikhoi was from the veld: wild plants and game. To preserve meat they salted, dried or smoked it. For smoking, they used wood from the surrounding areas, sometimes Rooibos. Sorrel was the main flavour used by the Khoikhoi, and buttermilk one of their favourite foods.

To prepare your dish, smoke thin slices of ostrich in a smoker but replace the oak chips with rooibos twigs.

To prepare the buttermilk sauce, warm chopped sorrel bulbs, leaves and stems in buttermilk, leave overnight to thicken and strain the sorrel off.

Ingredients

6	ostrich steaks (approx. 100g each)
500g	loose rooibos tea

Sauce

300ml	buttermilk
2	cloves garlic, crushed
6	sorrel leaves, finely chopped
	salt and pepper to taste

Serves 6

Method

Place the ostrich steaks on the smoking rack in a smoker*. Wet the rooibos tea slightly and place in the smoker. Smoke for about 15-20 minutes. Remove from the smoker and cool to room temperature.

Slice each steak thinly and place on a plate.

*If you do not have a smoker, line a heavy-based saucepan with foil, sprinkle the wet tea on the base, place a cake rack over the tea and pack the steaks on the rack. Make sure there is enough space between the steaks for the smoke to circulate. Cover the pot and seal with foil. Bring the pot to heat – you will see some smoke escaping – turn off the heat and leave the pot until it has cooled down.

Sauce

Pour the buttermilk into a mixing bowl, add the rest of the ingredients and mix well.

Serve immediately over smoked ostrich.

Notes

Should you not want to go to the trouble of smoking the meat yourself, there are very good smoked ostrich products available.

To get the rooibos taste, make a very strong rooibos tea, reduce to an essence, drizzle the essence over the smoked meat, then the sorrel dressing and serve.

Annette Cowley Nel

Former Springbok Swimmer and Businesswoman

It was in the Mother City – in Blouberg to be specific – that this water-baby who won fame in swimming pools internationally started her love affair with gardens. She planted her sweetpeas far too close together in that very first house she bought straight out of studenthood, enjoying their messy abundance every spring – and so was born a passion for creating a "plentiful" garden.

The homely Cowley Nel is a far cry from the young woman who was awarded Springbok colours for swimming for three consecutive years from 1982, and who went on to become famous for holding six national titles two years in a row. Her list of swimming titles during the 1980s in Britain and the US is impressive, but nature called – literally – and since her return home to South Africa in 1988, she's been driven by her love of creating "special spaces".

Today Cowley Nel is co-owner of a marketing and brand-positioning business specialising in luxury brands – but she still loves to plant those sweetpeas. "I need to be close to nature and love the changing of the seasons. It all started with the sweetpeas, and now it's more like a passion for herbs, vegetables and artichokes – and anything to do with cooking!"

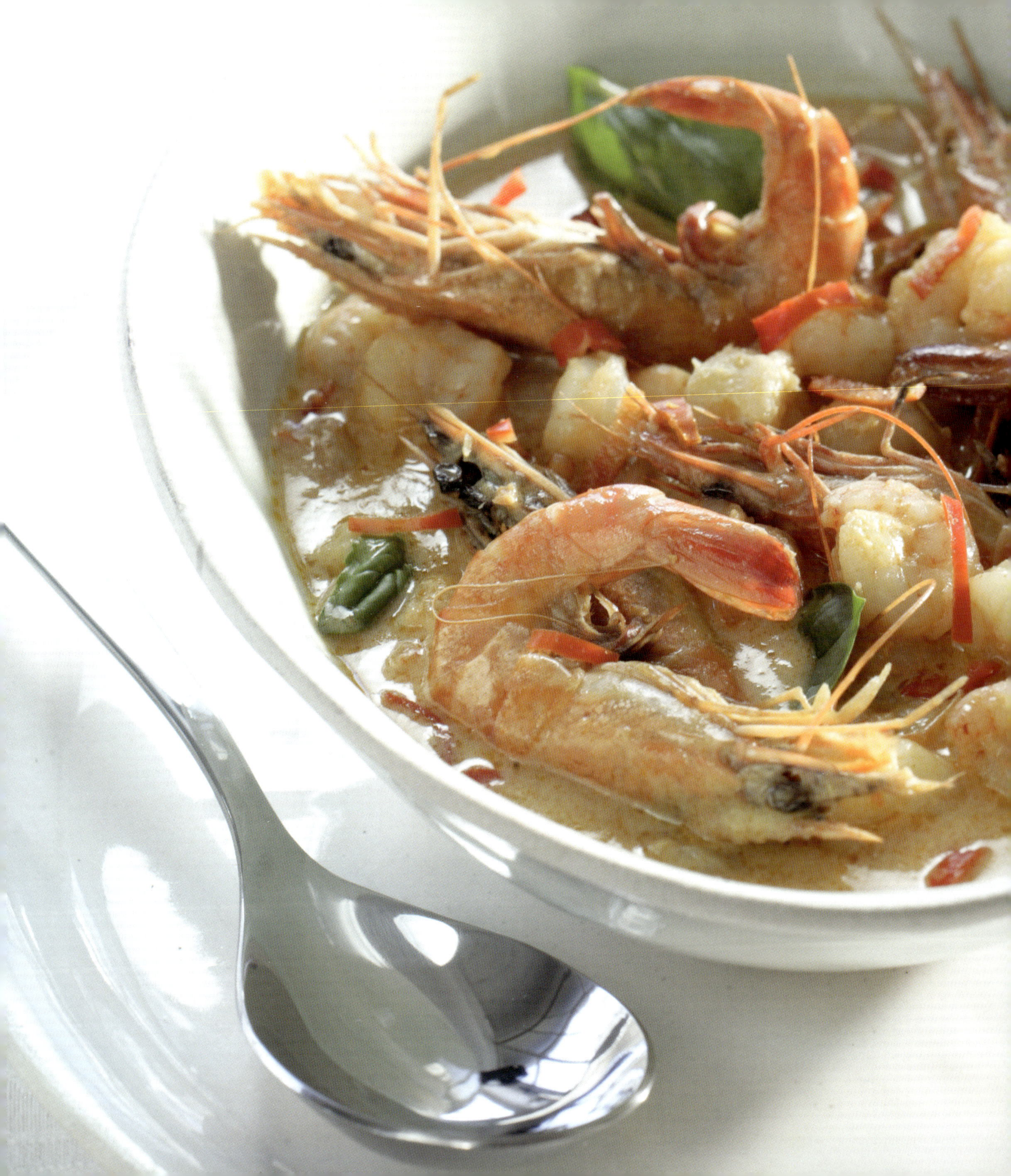

Chuchi Goong
(King Prawns in Red Curry)

The chef at the Banyan Tree Spa in the Seychelles, where we spent our tenth wedding anniversary, gave me this recipe. It's very decadent, a real treat – and very easy to make!

Ingredients

300g	prawns
400g	(2 cups) coconut milk
70g	red chillis, sliced
10g	fish sauce
5g	palm sugar
2g	basil leaves
2g	lime leaves
100g	red curry paste

Serves 4

Method

Sauté the red curry in oil with 1 cup coconut milk.

Then add second cup coconut milk, continue stirring until it boils, and add prawns.

Add lime leaves, then fish sauce and palm sugar.

Simmer for another 3-5 minutes.

Serve topped with basil leaves and slices of red chilli.

FW and Elita de Klerk

*Former President of South Africa
and Nobel Laureate*

Mr De Klerk made international history when, on February 2 1990, he lifted the 30-year ban on leading anti-apartheid group, and now the country's ruling party, the African National Congress. Nine days later on 11 February, F W de Klerk freed South Africa's most famous political prisoner, Nelson Mandela, opening the way to a peaceful democracy that most people across the world never believed possible. Three years later, with Mandela, De Klerk accepted the Nobel Peace Prize for his role in ending apartheid.

As leader of the National Party, of which he was a stalwart from 1972, De Klerk watched his party lose to the ANC in the country's historic first democratic election. He became one of two executive Deputy Presidents, a post he held until mid-1996 when his party withdrew from the Government of National Unity. He has been awarded numerous honorary degrees and several international awards. In September 1997, De Klerk bid goodbye to active politics, and has now written his autobiography, *"The Last Trek – A New Beginning"*.

De Klerk's unique experience in democratic change, and his eagerness to serve the causes of national reconciliation and constitutional democracy, still take him around the world.

At home on his farm about 60km from Cape Town where he lives with his wife Elita, De Klerk is however breaking more new ground – he's set to produce his own wine.

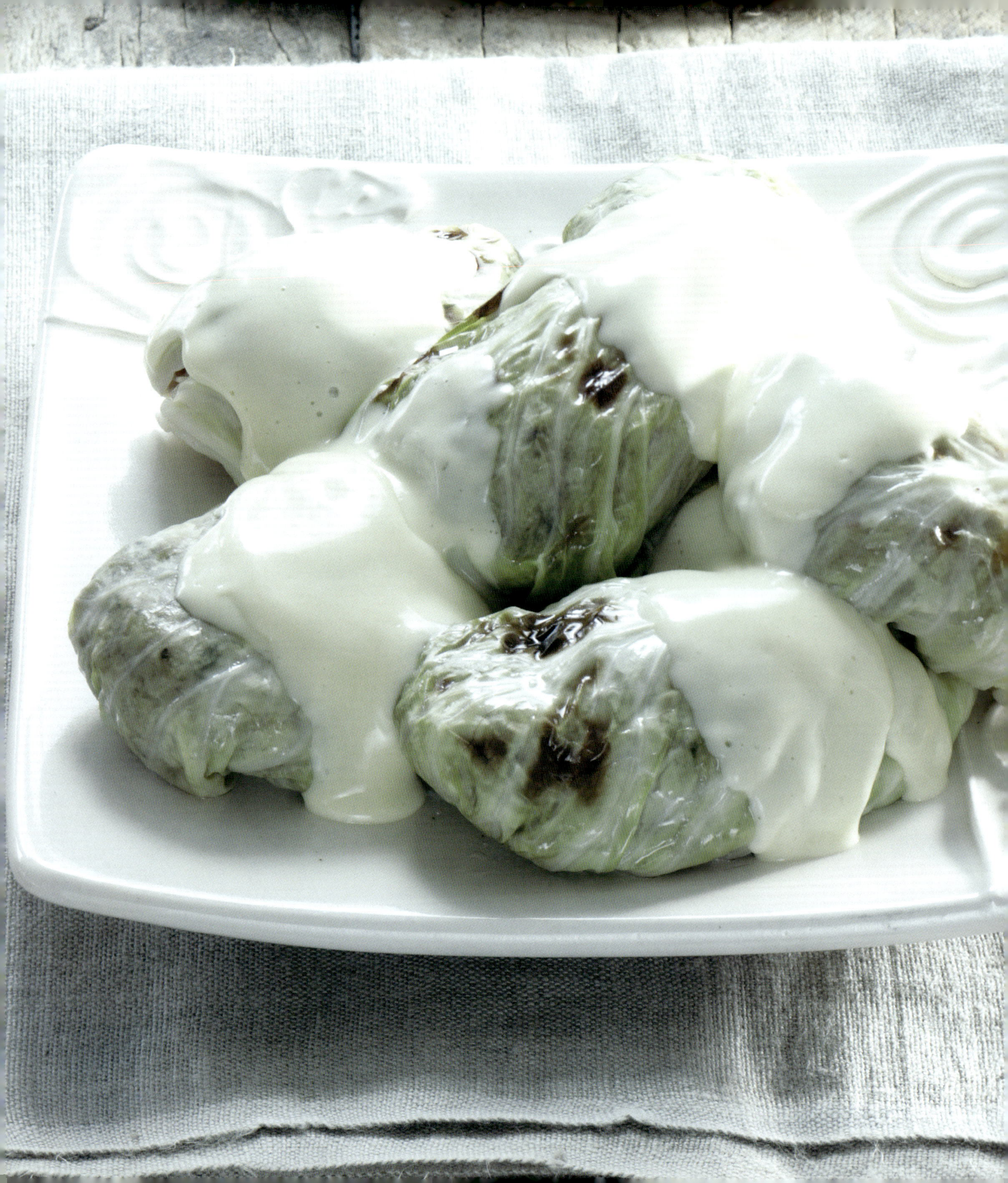

Lakhano Dolmades
(Stuffed Cabbage Leaves)

This delicious Greek dish in egg and lemon sauce can give that extra zing if you add some lemon zest to the sauce just before serving.

Ingredients

1	white cabbage, about 1kg in weight
200g	ground (minced) beef
200g	ground (minced) pork
200g	cooked rice
2	tomatoes, diced
1	onion, grated
½	bunch flat-leaved parsley, finely chopped
½	bunch dill, finely chopped
2	sprigs of mint, finely chopped
200ml	Greek extra virgin olive oil
	salt
	freshly ground black pepper

Sauce

30g	butter
15ml	all-purpose flour
2	eggs
	juice of 2 lemons

Serves 4-6

Method

Wash the cabbage and place whole in a saucepan filled with water. Add a pinch of salt and blanch for 5 minutes. Then separate into individual leaves and cut out the thick bit of stalk.

Place the ground meats in a bowl and mix thoroughly with the rice, tomatoes, onions, parsley, dill, mint, olive oil, salt and pepper.

Place a tablespoonful of the mixture at a time on a cabbage leaf, tuck in the ends and roll up firmly.

Lay the rolls in a saucepan tightly packed together and cover with an upturned plate.

Fill the pan with water and simmer for 40 minutes over a low heat. Drain, reserving the liquid, and keep the dolmades warm.

Sauce

Melt the butter in a small saucepan and lightly brown the flour.

Pour in just under 1 cup/200ml of the reserved liquid and bring to the boil for a moment.

Lightly beat the eggs in a bowl, and then slowly add the lemon juice, stirring constantly.

Stir this mixture into the melted butter and flour. Heat slowly (do not allow to boil), stirring constantly until the sauce thickens.

Pour over the rolled-up cabbage leaves and allow to stand for a few minutes.

Serve hot with freshly baked white bread.

Notes

This dish can work very well as a vegetarian dish by replacing the 200g ground beef with the same amount of cooked lentils, and the 200g ground pork with 200g mixed chopped nuts.

Denise Dogon

Property Dynamo

Denise Dogon's success lies in going the extra mile and making her individual mark. This dynamic, unstoppable lady lives daily by her mantra: "If it is meant to be, it is up to me!"

Dogon was an extremely successful realtor on Cape Town's desirable Atlantic Seaboard for more than 30 years, during which time she assisted the companies she worked for with their growth. In 2002, she took the plunge and went solo, establishing DG Properties – and was determined to offer a property company with a difference. As a result of a lifetime of travel and a sophisticated approach, she branded the DG name very differently from how the other property companies were doing it in South Africa. "Although branding is very important, our ultimate success is due to hard work, delivering great service and remembering that you are only as good as your last sale".

Both her sales and leadership style display a no-nonsense attitude. "I tend to confront things head-on and I always try to act with integrity." When she does take a break, it's likely to be in New York, her favourite place in the world. Time is a commodity in short supply in her business, and although she'd like to have more time to indulge her passion for jazz, it is ultimately her clients who always come first.

The satisfaction of a happy buyer is what Dogon likes best about the business, one which hooked her as a 23-year-old newlywed rookie, who sold her first property in the first week on the job. Property selling for Dogon was a natural instinct – she was born with it!

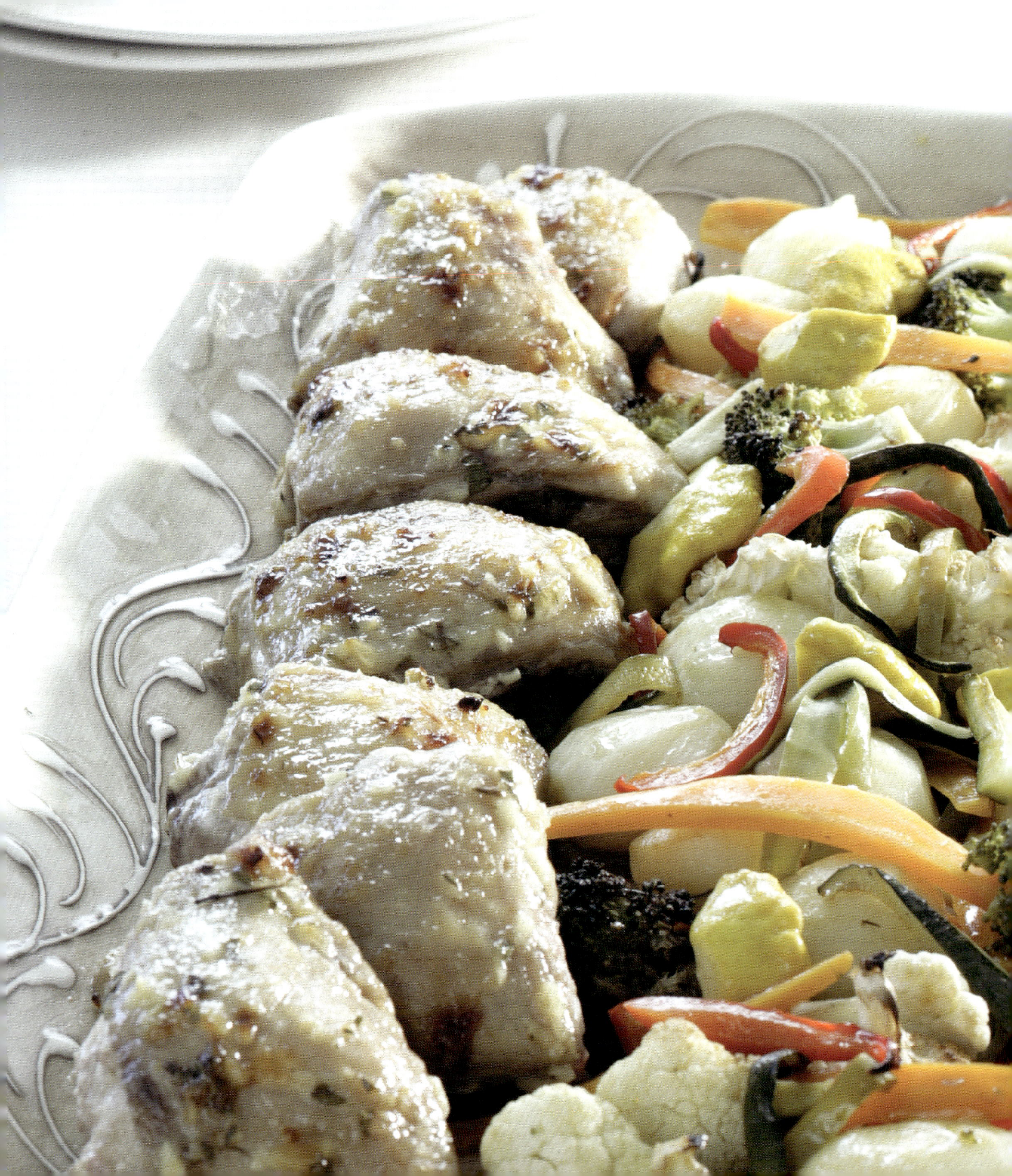

Chicken with Herb & Lemon Marinade and Grilled Vegetables

Spending time with my family is vitally important and precious to me, and this is the one meal that is thoroughly enjoyed by my children, my husband and myself from start to finish... it's the kind of meal that brings family and friends together.

Ingredients

10	pieces of chicken
	salt and freshly ground black pepper

Marinade

60ml	lemon juice
125ml	mayonnaise
2.5ml	crushed garlic
15ml	honey
2.5ml	dried mixed herbs

Grilled vegetables

1	small head of cauliflower, broken into florets
1	small head of broccoli, broken into florets
200g	baby marrows
1	large onion, sliced
200g	carrots, sliced
500g	baby potatoes
200g	patty pans
1	green pepper, diced
	olive oil
	vegetable seasoning to taste
	soya sauce

Serves 4-6

Method

Preheat the oven to 160°C.

Wash the chicken pieces and season lightly with the salt and pepper. Place in an ovenproof dish.

Mix all the marinade ingredients together and pour over the chicken pieces. Place in the oven and roast until the chicken is done, baste occasionally with the marinade.

When cooked, remove from the oven and keep warm.

Parboil the carrots and baby potatoes first until they are just done.

Heat a large saucepan and add a little olive oil.

Place all the vegetables in the saucepan and par cook until al dente.

Remove the vegetables from the stove and place in an ovenproof dish with a sprinkling of vegetable seasoning and soya sauce.

Place them under the grill on the middle rack (after you have removed the chicken) and grill until just cooked.

Serve with a green salad.

Zillian Dube

Acclaimed South African Actress

Making it big in Hollywood is exactly what acclaimed South African actress Lillian Dube has done – without leaving her beloved home country. She's rubbed shoulders with film greats James Earl Jones and Charles Dutton, and her movie *Cape of Good Hope*, in which she played Mama, made it as a New York Times Critics Pick in 2004. But this outstanding and distinguished actress is all home-grown, and her biggest fan base is definitely right here in South Africa where she has been a mainstay of the entertainment industry for 20 years.

Whether its television, film or theatre, Dube has proved that local stars don't need to leave South Africa to make it big in Hollywood. This star of the stage and big screen prides herself on staying close to her roots, committing herself to help fight some of the major scourges threatening South African society today – HIV/Aids, drug abuse and diabetes.

Since 1994, her movie line-up has included *A Good Man in Africa* and *Cry, the Beloved Country*, but she's probably best known locally as Sister Bettina on *Soul City*, and Masebobe in *Generations*. Other than Hollywood, Dube has also shown off her talents in Scotland and Germany, where she appeared in *Curl Up and Dye*.

She may have notched up a string of awards for her talents, but her role as a public and motivational speaker has endeared her to many more than only those she has entertained. Dube is a true South African superstar.

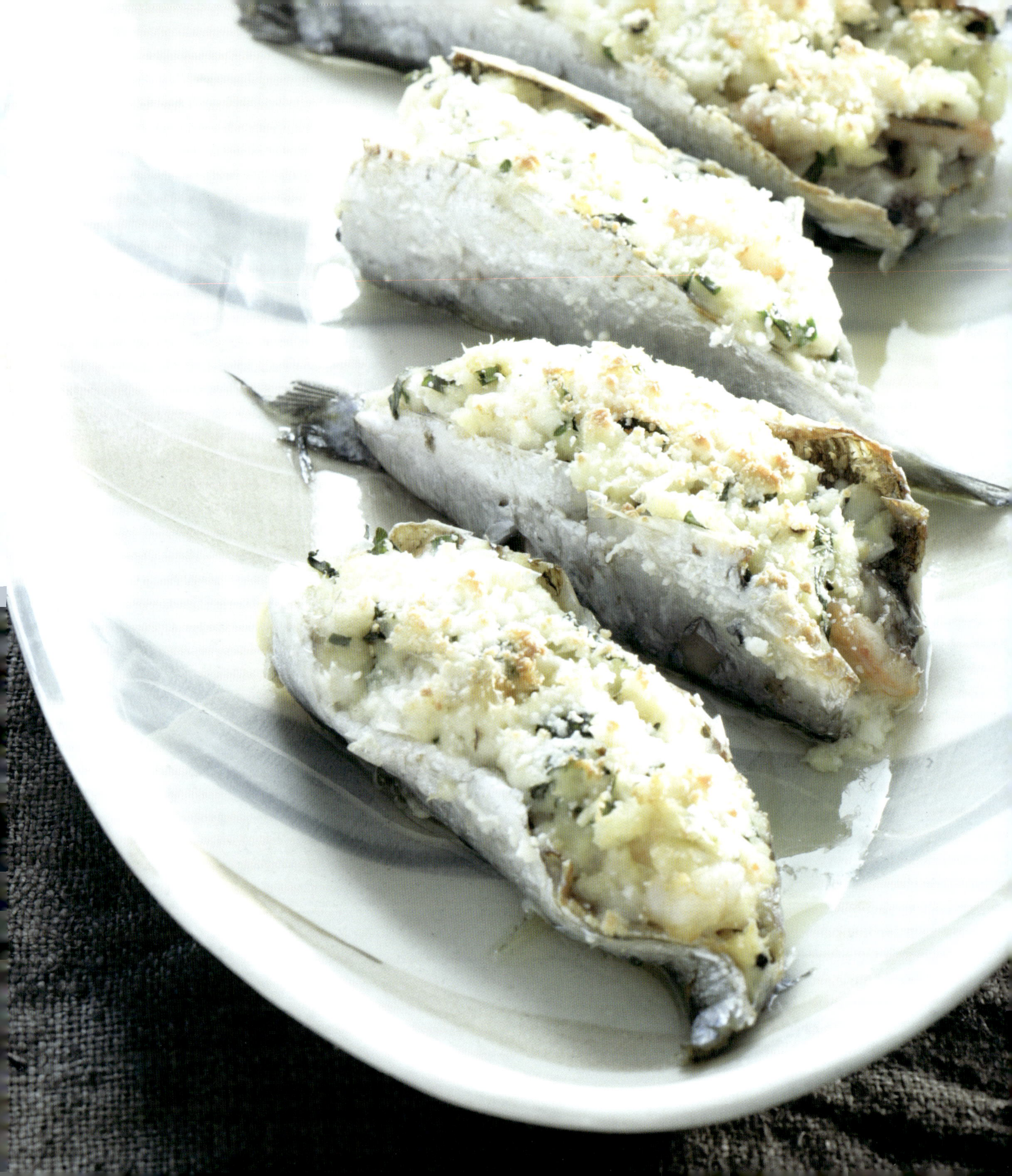

Lillian's Sardines

This is a very special dish. Lillian gave it to us as a dish for Lent, but it is ideal for any time of the year. I have found that this dish works well on a fire. Wrap the fish in foil and "bake" on the fire or in a weber.

Ingredients

12	fresh sardines
40ml	olive oil
100g	hake or any other firm-fleshed fish
600g	cooked medium prawns, peeled, deveined and chopped
100ml	cooked rice
3	cloves garlic, crushed
15ml	fresh mint, chopped
15ml	chives, chopped
15ml	basil, chopped
30ml	parmesan cheese, grated
10ml	lemon juice
1	egg, lightly beaten
30ml	breadcrumbs
	salt and black pepper to taste

Serves 6 as a starter or 4 as a main course

Method

Preheat the oven to 180°C. Lightly grease a rectangular ovenproof dish.

Remove the heads and tails of the sardines, make a slit along the underside of the belly and remove the intestines and backbone. Rinse under cold running water and pat dry. Lay the sardines flat skin-side down.

Heat 10ml of the olive oil in a frying pan, fry the hake (until just cooked, be careful not to fry too brown.

Flake the fish and mix with the prawns, rice, garlic, mint, chives, basil, parmesan and lemon juice. Adjust the seasoning and stir in the lightly beaten egg.

Divide the filling among the sardines and fill each sardine's belly cavity with the mixture. Sprinkle the breadcrumbs on each filled fish and place in the ovenproof dish (on their backs with the filling facing up).

Drizzle with olive oil and bake for 20-25 minutes or until golden.

Notes

Drizzle with lemon juice and serve immediately with a green salad.

Billy Gallagher

Director of Public Relations and
Communications, Southern Sun Hotel

Dr Bill Gallagher has faced adversity head-on, proving that there is definitely life – and a full one at that – after being shot in the spine and left a quadriplegic during a hijacking in 2000.

From 1996 to 2000, this world-renowned chef was president of the World Association of Cooks Societies, and he's been honoured with culinary awards in more than 20 countries.

Clearly standing out from his long list of achievements is his World Cooks Tour for the Hunger Worldwide Project, which in 1993 brought 100 chefs from 30 countries to Africa to raise R500 000 for Operation Hunger and The Valley Trust. In 2003, he repeated the effort, with 150 chefs this time, and raised an astonishing R1.3 million for the African Feeding Scheme and Heartbeat.

Two years later, Gallagher got a Lifetime Achievement Award for services to the hospitality industry from *Eat Out* Magazine (South Africa), and the following year, in 2006, received a second Lifetime Achievement Award, this time from the World Association of Chefs Societies. The same year he was also presented with the inaugural Golden Vine Award in recognition of his promotion of the South African wine industry.

Today Gallagher has "learnt to do things differently". He heads up public relations and communication for the Southern Sun Group, but is still responsible for casino food and beverage operations.

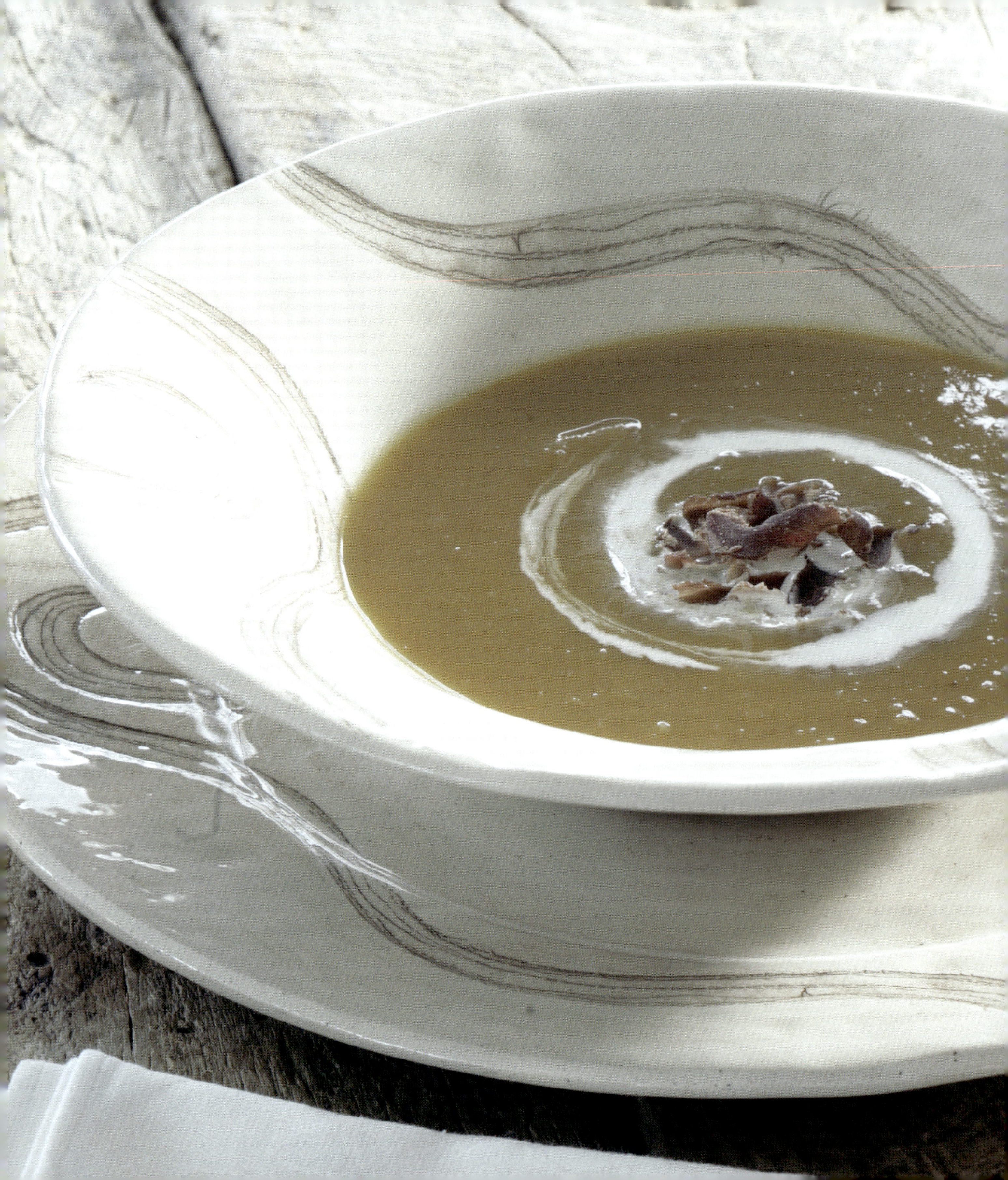

Pumpkin and Biltong Soup

As a *pièce de résistance*, serve in hollowed out baby pumpkins, which have been heated in the oven.

Ingredients

1kg	pumpkin
500ml	chicken stock
250ml	water
1	chopped onion
2	cloves crushed garlic
125ml	cream
15ml	lemon juice
	biltong shavings to garnish

Serves 4

Method

Peel pumpkin and dice into small chunks.

Combine pumpkin in a large saucepan with stock, water, onion, and garlic.

Bring to the boil, reduce heat to low and simmer for 20 minutes or until pumpkin is tender.

Transfer mixture to food processor or blender and process until smooth.

Return the soup to the saucepan. Now, add the cream and lemon juice to the soup, simmer gently for a further four to five minutes.

Check for seasoning and garnish with biltong shavings.

Serve immediately.

Notes

For a smoky/roasted flavour: roast the pumpkin in preheated oven at 180°C until the pumpkin is just cooked. Then put it into the saucepan with the other ingredients, bring to the boil, and proceed as per the recipe.

Gwen Gill

Veteran Social Writer

Grande dame of the social circuit, Gwen Gill has probably done more than any other print journalist in the country to build a South African cult of celebrity. Even if that means most people are afraid of her – and that goes for her own family members too. Gill is frank that it goes with the territory, that people are wary of sharing intimate details with her because of what she might, or might not say in her *Sunday Times* weekly column, read avidly by millions of people.

Of course there's the other downside – whether she's being well treated only because of who she is. But Gill says that celebrities make themselves, and if they're worth writing about, she will – and aspiration is all-important.

Since she started at the *Sunday Times* as an editorial secretary in 1971, Gill has become a master of re-invention; from the paper's first TV critic in the 1970s, she became an award-winning consumer columnist, before moving on to chronicle the parties, the fashions, the food and the goings-on of the country's rich and famous – not always in very flattering terms.

What most people don't know is that under the quick wit and sharply critical eye lurks a down-to-earth, amiable mother and grandmother who's happy as long as she has her "things around her". And that includes her collection of 350 cookbooks because Gill is an enthusiastic cook and regular correspondent on the *food24.com* website.

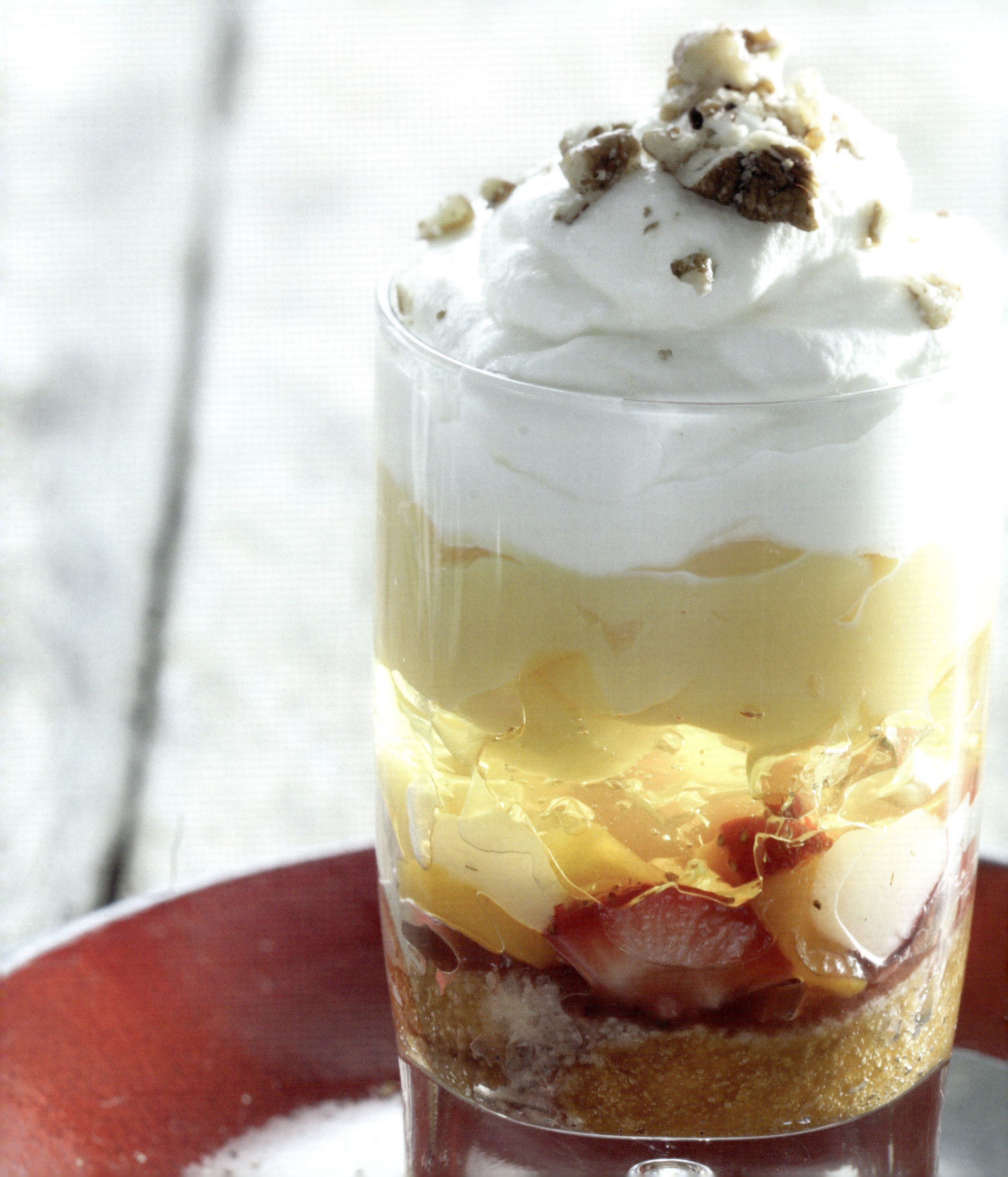

My Mum's Trashy but Terrific Trifle

A trifle is always a winner – it can be dressed up and made grand or just served as food for the soul. I like it the day after when everything is mushy – I don't get it often as everyone has seconds!

Ingredients

1	jam swiss roll, cut into slices
	strawberry jam
30ml	sherry or port (or whatever you are legally supposed to call it these days)
1	tin fruit salad or sliced peaches, preferably canned in fruit juice
1	orange or lemon jelly
500ml	custard made from custard powder (bought is too runny and made from scratch is too fussy)
2	ripe bananas (optional)
	whipping cream
	a few chopped nuts or grated chocolate for topping

Serves 8

Method

Smear cake slices with jam and put in a glass bowl.

Sprinkle the booze over.

Put drained fruit on top.

Make up jelly, using boiling water and the juice from the tinned fruit, as directed on jelly packet. Allow to set (about two hours).

Make custard according to directions. Allow to cool a bit so it won't melt jelly.

Slice bananas (if using) and stir into custard. Pour onto trifle and put the dish in the fridge for a few hours or overnight.

Notes

Just before your guests arrive, whip cream, spread on top of trifle and scatter on chopped nuts or chocolate, or whole very ripe and sweet strawberries.

Pam Golding

*Founding Director of Business Against Crime
Western Cape and ultimate "home bird"*

Pam Golding's green "For Sale" signs might have made her a household name among property buyers and sellers, but the example she's set for South African women in business must surely outstrip everything else. Not many people know that this top-notch company chairperson was a housewife and mother who, more than 30 years ago, took the giant leap of starting her own business.

The rewards have been phenomenal, but she well remembers her humble beginnings – "with the sale of just one property, and during a recession at that". Today you'll see her at all the top-end functions, but what's really closest to Golding's heart is family, which she says is the foundation of life. Her descriptions of family celebrations say it all: "Family events are celebrated with friends of all ages, and sometimes end with a soiree round the piano with Cecil, a jazz pianist, on the keyboard."

Golding is indeed a high-profile, award-winning businesswoman and property tycoon, but at home she's just Pam, the "wife, mother and grandmother sharing their lovely home in Constantia". She's a home bird and earth mother whose warmth and charm, passion for action and abundant enthusiasm encompasses all aspects of her life – work and play.

Golding's reminder to women is that "the hand that rocks the cradle is the hand that rules the world. Strive to achieve" she urges, "but never neglect the hearth".

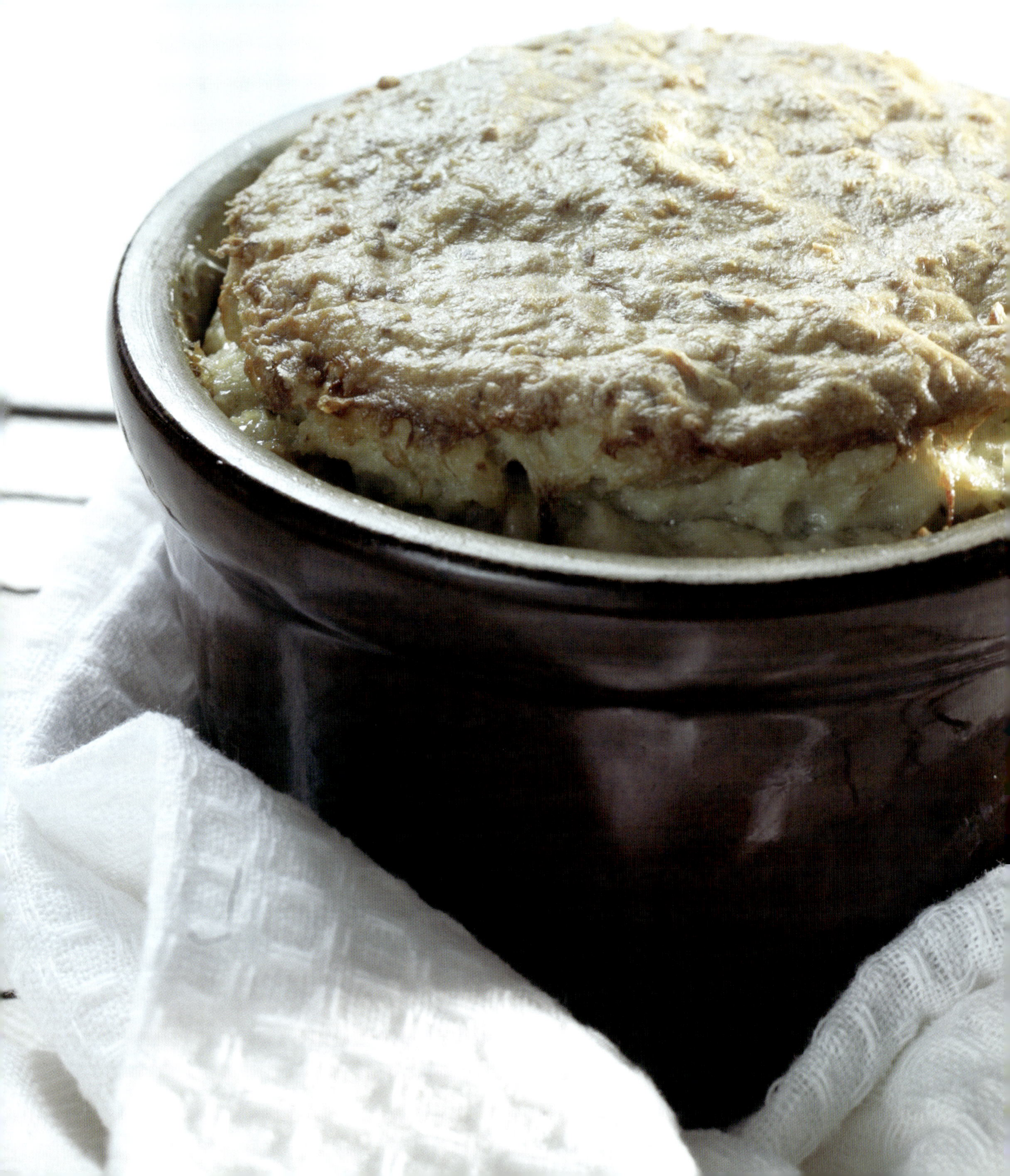

Pam Golding's Favourite Fish Soufflé

Most people are intimidated by a soufflé – but it is one of the easiest dishes to make. Just remember to serve it immediately to get the total effect. Individual soufflés can be made, rested, removed from the dariole mould and baked again – you can then call it a twice-baked soufflé.

Ingredients

500g	skinned fish fillets
500ml	milk
1	bay leaf
6	peppercorns
4	sprigs of parsley
½	onion, sliced
30g	(30ml) butter
30ml	cake flour
1ml	dry English mustard
2ml	salt
3	eggs separated
	milled black pepper

Serves 4

Method

Preheat the oven to 150°C. Butter a soufflé dish.

In a wide saucepan, heat the milk with the bay leaf, peppercorns, parsley and a few onion rings.

Add the fish, cover and poach very gently until cooked. Remove from pan, flake and set aside.

Strain and reserve the poaching liquid to use in the sauce.

Sauce

In a clean saucepan melt the butter, remove from the heat and blend in the flour and mustard, then add the poaching liquid.

Season with salt and pepper and stir over high heat until the sauce is smooth and thickened.

Remove from the heat, beat in the egg yolks, then gently fold in the flaked fish. Allow the mixture to cool, then whisk the egg white stiffly and fold in.

Pour the mixture into the soufflé dish and bake for 30 minutes.

Serve immediately with a fresh salad.

Dr Patricia Gorvalla

Managing Director of the Gorvalla Group of Companies and Founding Director of Business Against Crime Western Cape

From pre-schools to women's clubs, and educational institutions to some of the country's most prominent business interests, Dr Patricia Gorvalla has a list of directorships, trusteeships and memberships so long that it's difficult to imagine how she ever keeps up.

This managing director of the Gorvalla Group of Companies may be a septuagenarian, but she still holds her own as owner of the 11 initiatives that fall under the umbrella of her company.

Wherever there is talk about empowerment and the female high-flyers in South African business today, Gorvalla's name is sure to be there. In 2001, the Black Management Forum presented Gorvalla, a pioneer in the minibus transport service, with its Jubilee Award in recognition of her outstanding business career.

In all, this remarkable entrepreneur who proved that anything men can do, women can do equally well, has launched 14 businesses, accompanied the government on numerous trade missions, and has represented South Africa on the SA-United States Committee on Trade and Development.

Gorvalla is far too busy being a success to concern herself with sexist attitudes, and suggests that other women keen to follow her example up the ladder to achievement should acquire the necessary knowledge and skills in an area they find stimulating and exciting. And as for advice on bringing up children – she has three daughters: "Give your children quality time, and you can burn the candle at both ends after they're asleep."

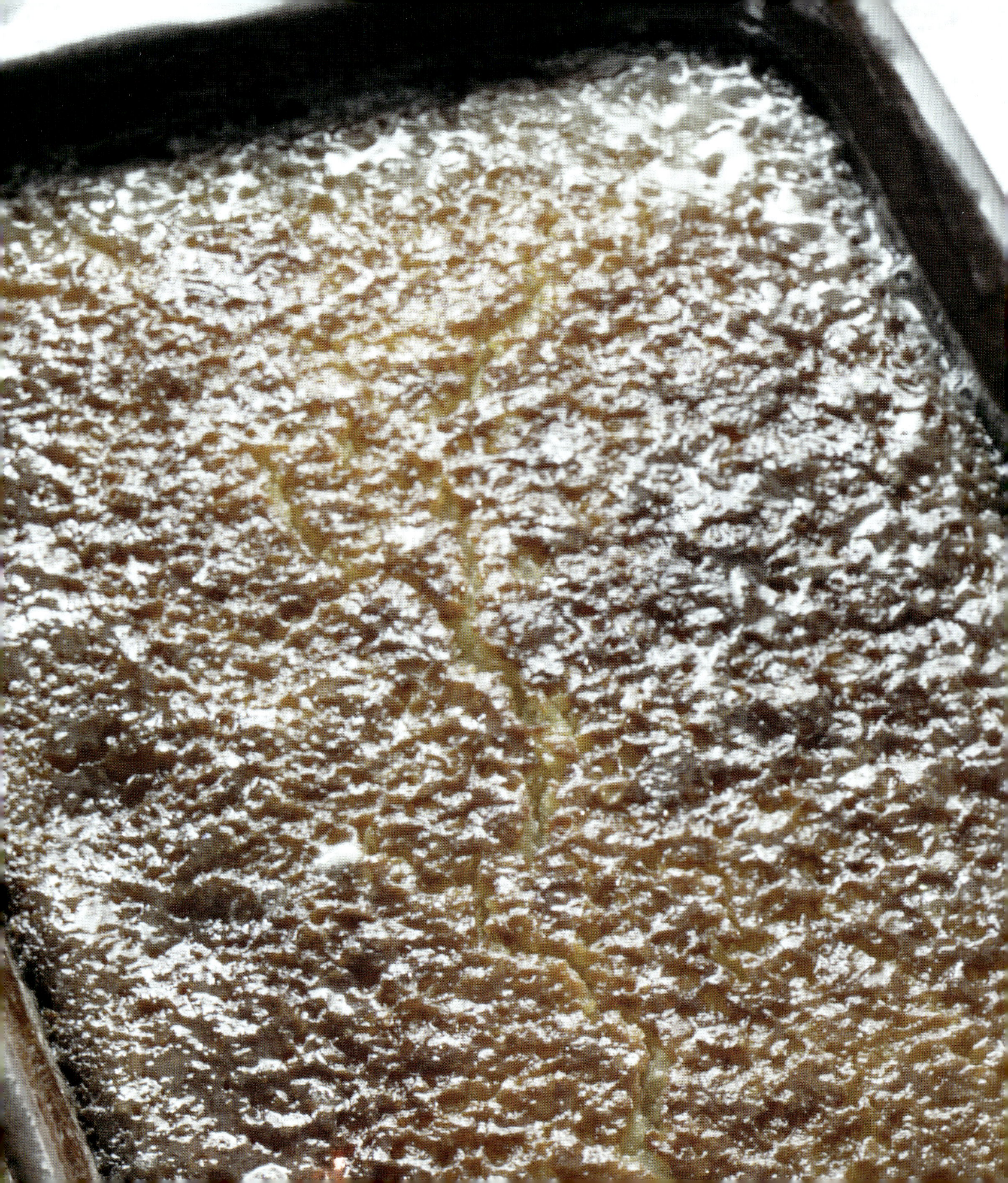

Malva Pudding

This is everyone's favourite recipe, I've discovered. They all love it, and I'm rather fond of it myself!

Ingredients

1	egg
250ml	sugar
15ml	smooth apricot jam
250ml	flour
5ml	bicarbonate of soda
	generous pinch of salt
15ml	butter
5ml	vinegar
125ml	milk
125ml	cream

Sauce

250ml	milk
250ml	cream
180g	butter
250ml	sugar
125ml	hot water

Serves 4-6

Method

Preheat the oven to 180°C.

Beat egg, sugar and jam together to a creamy consistency (about 15 minutes).

Sift flour, bicarb and salt into a bowl.

Melt butter and add vinegar.

Add milk and cream to egg mixture as well as the flour. Add vinegar and butter. Mix well.

Pour into a dish about 20cm in diameter, cover with foil and bake for 45 minutes to 1 hour. The pudding is cooked when it is a consistent rich-brown colour. If it is still pale in the centre on top, it will need a little longer.

Sauce

Melt together the ingredients for the sauce and pour over the pudding as it comes out of the oven. If you re-heat the pudding and it is slightly dry, pour over a little boiling water.

Notes

For an interesting twist – grate 125ml raw butternut into the mixture. This will give this favourite pudding a contemporary twist.

To jazz up the sauce replace the 125ml water with 125ml dry sherry – you may now take a bow!

Anthony and Olive Hamilton Russell

Owners of Hamilton Russell Vineyards and Southern Right Wines, Hermanus

Anthony Hamilton Russell creates wines "with personality", thanks to the incandescent beauty of the Hemel en Aarde Valley with its salty sea air from Walker Bay cooling the vineyards, and the smell of fynbos in the air. It's a place with "soul", which Hamilton Russell and his "farmer's wife" Olive call home, where he has won international acclaim for his Hamilton Russell Vineyards: Chardonnay and Pinot Noir.

When he bought the vineyard from his father Tim in 1994, it was with big plans to help make South African wines known around the world, and to put the wines of Hamilton Russell vineyards on the map internationally. He wanted to produce wines with a real sense of place – the place being that splendid valley which, the story goes, has ley lines running through it making it especially spiritual. That sense of place is reinforced by only working with estate-grown grapes, and he's even turned his hand to drying imported French oak right in the vineyard for shipping back to France to be fashioned into barrels.

It's hardly surprising then that he's helped secure the environment that has made his wines famous, creating a pristine large private fynbos reserve which is home to a variety of wildlife. Living by his belief that "the process of making wines is all-embracing" is clearly what Hamilton Russell does best.

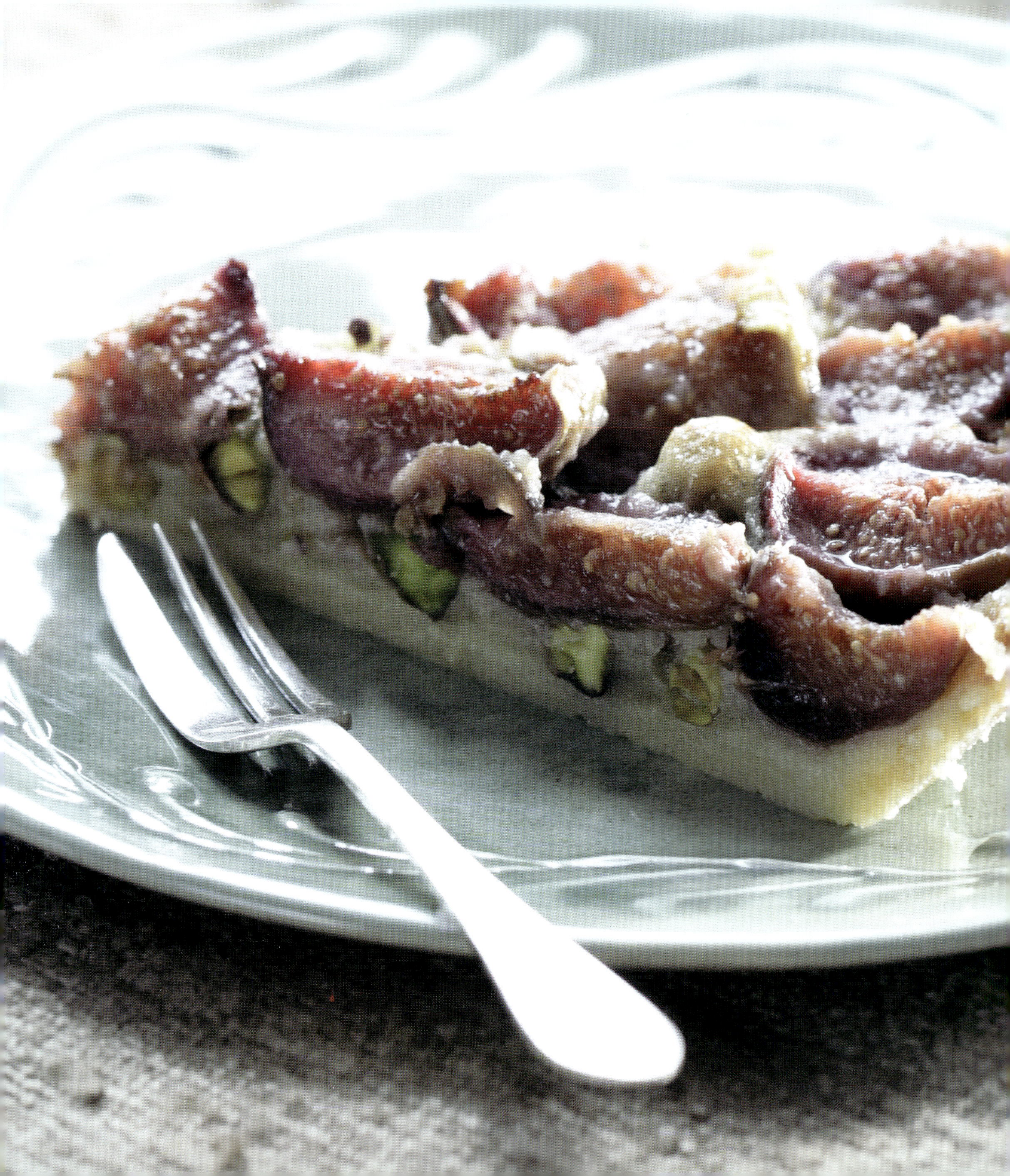

Fig and Pistachio Tart

Should you not be able to find fresh figs for this recipe – rehydrate dried figs in rooibos tea, remove from the tea, dry with a kitchen towel, slice and use in the tart.

Ingredients

Pastry

120g	butter
2	egg yolks
80g	icing sugar
250g	cake flour
	pinch of salt

Filling

200g	butter
200g	icing sugar
2	large eggs
150g	pistachios, unsalted, shelled and peeled
50g	cake flour
7-8	ripe figs
15g	icing sugar, for sprinkling
60g	fynbos honey, melted
250ml	double cream Greek yoghurt
10	sour figs

Serves 4-6

Method

Pastry

Preheat oven to 150°C, and place oven rack in middle slot.

Cream butter in a mixer, add egg yolks, icing sugar and salt, and continue to blend until smooth and creamy.

Sift flour and add. Mix until a ball of pastry is formed. Wrap in cling film and leave to rest in fridge for one hour.

Roll pastry out to a thickness of about 2-3mm.

Spray a loose-bottom tart pan with 'spray & cook', and carefully line with pastry. Pierce pastry base several times with a fork.

Bake blind for 40 minutes.

Filling

Cream the butter and sugar in a food processor.

Add eggs, and once fully incorporated, add nuts and flour.

Smooth the butter mixture over pastry base.

Quarter each fig, and place around the inside edge of the pastry. Half the remaining quarters, and place in a circle inside the first round of figs. Place a horizontal round slice in the centre.

Sift icing sugar over tart, and bake for about 30 minutes, until golden brown.

Pour melted honey over tart as soon as it is removed from the oven – starting at centre of tart and pouring in an outwards spiral.

Once tart has cooled on a cooling rack, remove from tart pan (you don't have to slide it off).

Squeeze syrup from sour figs, and mix with yoghurt.

Serve with yoghurt and sour fig sauce.

Susan Huxter and Margot Janse

Owner and Executive Chef,
Le Quartier Francais, Franschhoek

Local is definitely lekker for Franschhoek's world-renowned hotelier Susan Huxter and executive chef Margot Janse, whose joint "girl power" – along with the third cog in their all woman wheel, wine fundi and garagiste winemaker, GM Linda Coltart, has put the Cape Winelands town firmly on the international map.

In 1996, Huxter took a chance on her then Sous Chef, promoting Janse to Executive Chef and opening the way for the superlative experience: at the tasting room, cutting edge cuisine; and great bistro food next door. This, combined with great service, makes for cuisine that people travel from far and wide to enjoy.

Their mantelpiece must surely be overflowing with awards they've gathered, both locally and internationally, but still the pair has never lost their appreciation for the freshness and variety of what's right on their doorstep. Janse says Franschhoek offers the most amazing produce, and she loves nothing more than getting colanders full of black figs, berries or nettles from the local women. This year she won the prestigious inaugural Relais and Chateaux Rising Chef Trophy 2007, and Le Quartier Francais has for the third time been voted one of the World's Top 50 Restaurants (*Restaurant Magazine*, UK).

Their mutual admiration is almost tangible – Huxter says she's mystified at how Janse's wellspring of talent just keeps on flowing, while Janse praises Huxter for allowing her to shape her own creative path. Combined with their firm commitment to nurturing local talent, it's hardly surprising that these three women are constantly raising the bar with their innovative and creative energy.

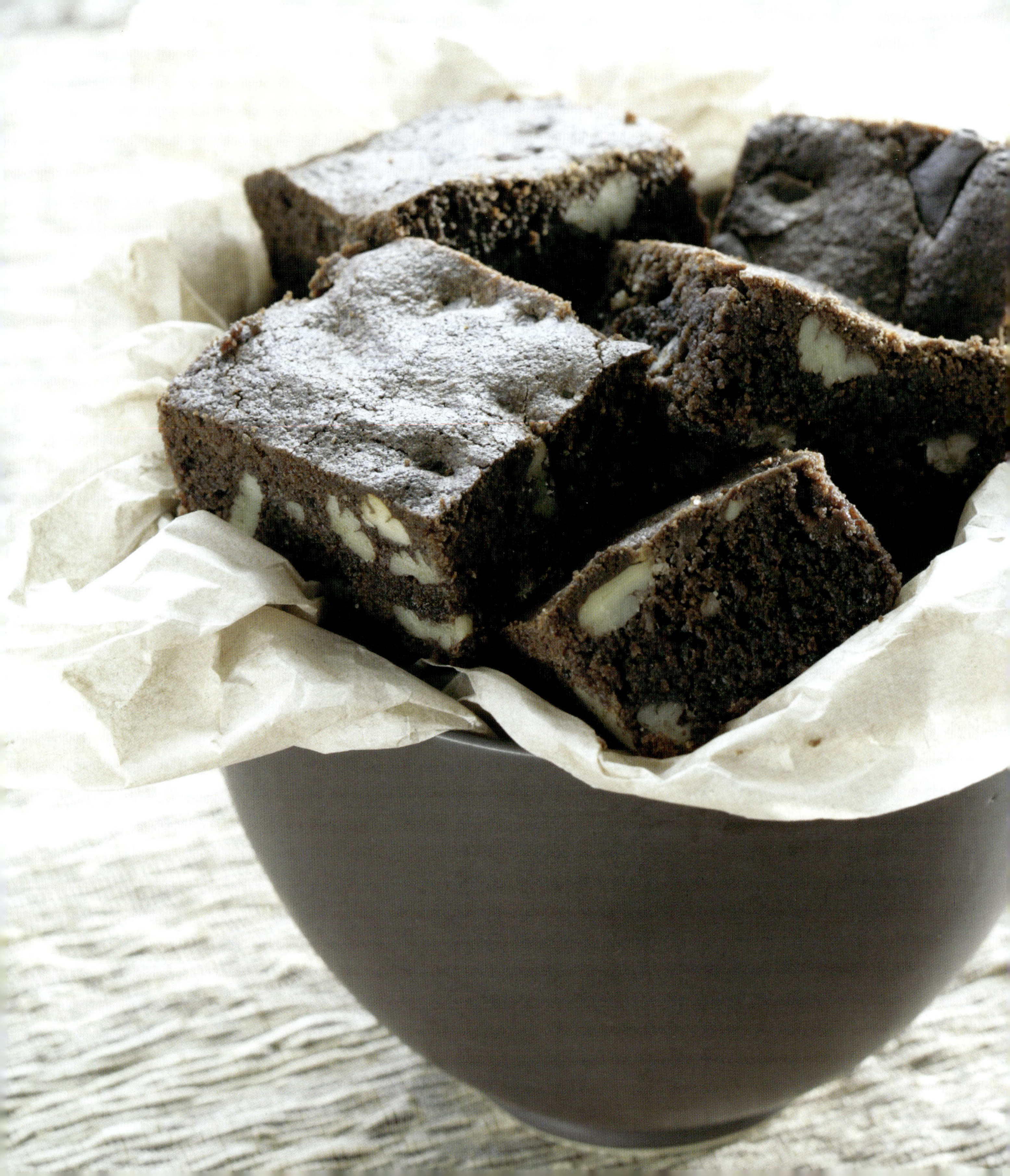

Choc-chip and Nut Brownies

I am a total chocoholic – one of those and I am done for! They are totally decadent and 'have to' eats. People love them and always want them on the next visit – but once I have baked them, I'm not sure if there will be any left for the guests!

Ingredients

125g	butter
125ml	castor sugar
3	eggs
125ml	cake flour
200g	cream cheese
200g	dark chocolate
600g	dark chocolate chips
500g	butter, unsalted
500ml	cake flour
250ml	cocoa powder
10	eggs, lightly beaten
200g	mixed nuts, chopped

Makes 24

Method

Preheat oven to 180°C.

Line a 50cm x 30cm oven tray with greaseproof paper.

Cream the butter and the sugar, add eggs one by one.

Mix in the flour and then the cream cheese. Set aside.

Melt 200g dark chocolate together with the butter in a bowl over simmering water. When melted add the sugar, then the flour, the beaten eggs and lastly the cream cheese mix. Then fold in the dark chocolate chips and the mixed nuts.

Pour mixture into tray and bake for 50 minutes.

When baked and while still hot, cut into squares.

Notes

When cooled totally, keep in an airtight container.

Vaughan Johnson

South African Wine Expert and Retailer

This proud informal ambassador of South Africa's wine industry has built an enviable reputation as one of the country's top wine experts – and one visit to his fine emporium proves why. Vaughan Johnson's Wine Shop is a must-see for both local and international visitors to one of Cape Town's prime tourist hotspots, the V&A Waterfront.

Johnson fought a well-documented five-year feud with the government over his application to trade on Sundays, won the battle, and today offers wine lovers a choice of 100 of the best of the 5 000 wines produced throughout South Africa. These are all, Johnson says, "exciting and satisfying wines, made by passionate winemakers". His promise is that he offers the finest quality Cape wines at the most reasonable prices.

Among the high-profile visitors to his wine shop have been United States Vice President Al Gore, former British Prime Minister Baroness Margaret Thatcher, and supermodel Naomi Campbell.

Travelling internationally and giving lectures and tastings of what the vines of the Cape have to offer, Johnson attributes his competitive edge to 30 years "as a winemaker, accountant and retailer" in the South African wine industry. He sells the best of the wines produced and bottled in the Western Cape, but takes care of clients with other tastes too.

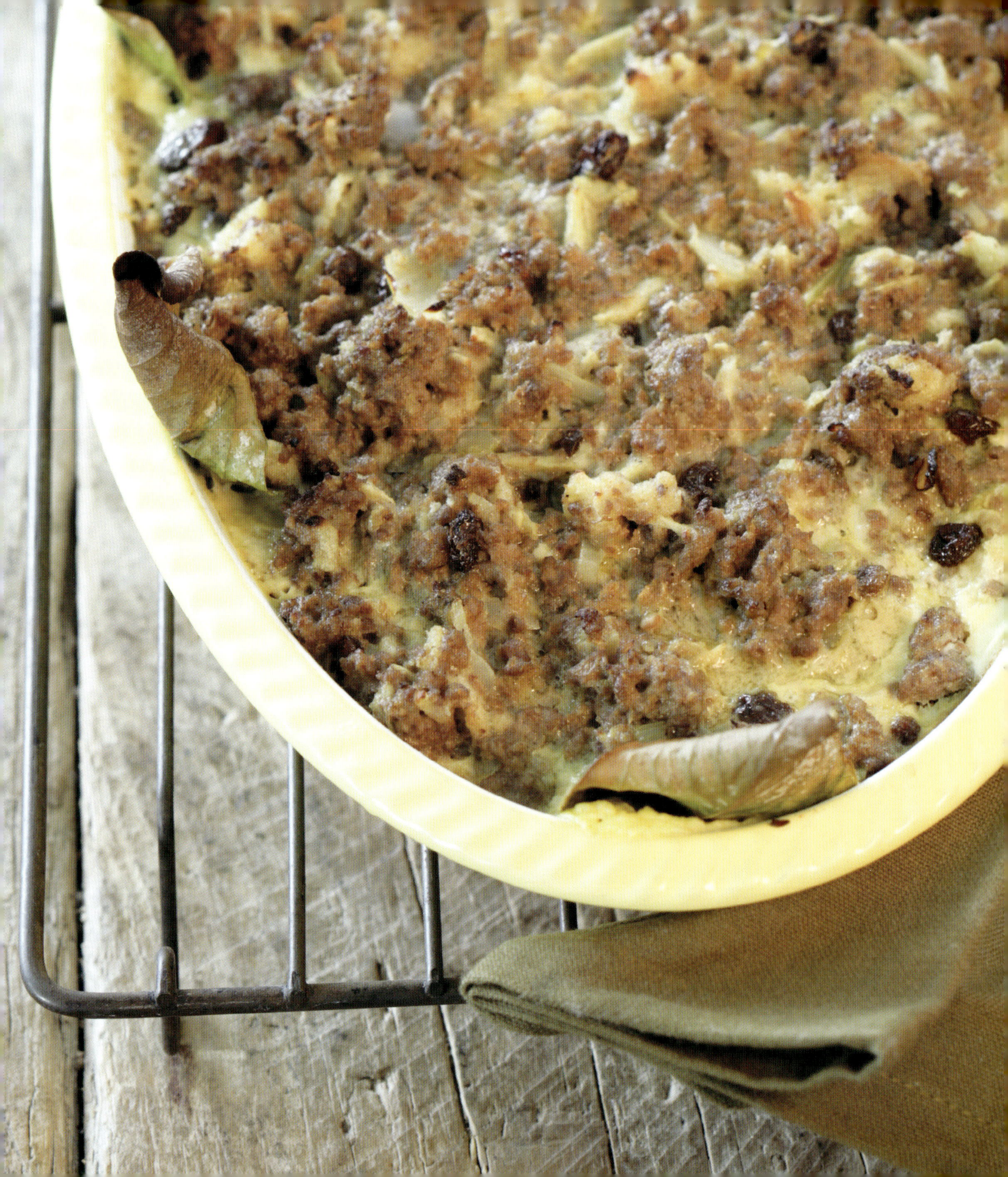

Bobotie

I have used this recipe from Gramadoelas restaurant in Johannesburg for years, by courtesy of the owners and my dear friend, Eduan Naude and Brian Shalkoff. Traditionally bobotie is made with minced mutton, but beef may also be used.

Ingredients

1	slice white bread, 3cm thick, broken into small bits
15ml	brown sugar
250ml	milk
5ml	salt
30ml	butter
2.5ml	freshly ground black pepper
30ml	oil
60ml	strained fresh lemon juice
1 kg	coarsely ground lean lamb
3	eggs
375ml	finely chopped onion
1	cooking apple, peeled, cored & finely grated
30ml	curry powder
125ml	seedless raisins
4	small fresh lemon leaves or bay leaves

Serves 4-6

Method

Preheat the oven to 180°C.

Combine the bread and milk in a small bowl and let the bread soak for 10 minutes.

In a heavy saucepan, melt the butter over moderate heat. When the foam subsides, add the oil, then the onions, stirring frequently.

Cook the onion until soft and translucent. Add the curry powder, sugar, salt and pepper, and stir for 2 minutes. Then add the lamb to the spices and stir. When browned, stir in the lemon juice and bring the mixture to the boil.

Drain the bread in a sieve set over a bowl and squeeze completely dry. Reserve the drained milk.

Add the bread, one of the eggs, the apple, raisins and almonds to the lamb. Stir or beat the mixture with a wooden spoon until the ingredients are well combined.

Taste for seasoning and add more salt, if desired.

Pack the lamb mixture loosely in an ovenproof baking dish. Tuck the lemon or bay leaves beneath the surface of the meat. With a whisk beat the remaining 2 eggs well with the reserved milk.

Pour this mixture slowly and evenly over the meat and bake on the middle rack of the oven for 10 minutes until the surface has browned and feels firm to the touch.

Notes

Serve directly from the baking dish as soon as it has been removed from the oven – with yellow raisin rice.

Basetsana Kumalo

*Television Personality and
Former Miss South Africa*

Beauty, brains and benevolence combine in the dynamic package that is Basetsana Kumalo, South Africa's second black Miss SA, turned glamorous TV personality and successful businesswoman.

Kumalo, who grew up in Soweto, is surely the perfect national role-model.

During her reign as Miss SA – she went on to be named first runner-up in the Miss World Pageant – Kumalo laid the groundwork for her community commitment which is still an intrinsic part of her life today. Also during her reign, she became a presenter of popular entertainment and lifestyle magazine programme *Top Billing*, later moving up to become the programme's producer and then co-owner of Tswelopele Productions, which produces the show.

Not content with being a best-dressed model for beautiful clothes, in 2000 Kumalo launched her own clothing range, distributed by Ackermans. The next year, she persuaded the company to give away clothes worth R1 million to 50 children's homes and non-government organisations across South Africa.

Kumalo's interview list is a 'who's who' of the world's rich and famous, and has shared her TV show with Nelson Mandela, Michael Jackson, Gloria Estefan, Elizabeth Hurley, the BeeGees, Sting, Oprah, Samuel L Jackson and Richard Branson, to name just a few. But fame hasn't gone to this glamour girl's head, and once a month on a Saturday you'll still find her visiting children in the cancer ward at Chris Hani Baragwanath Hospital.

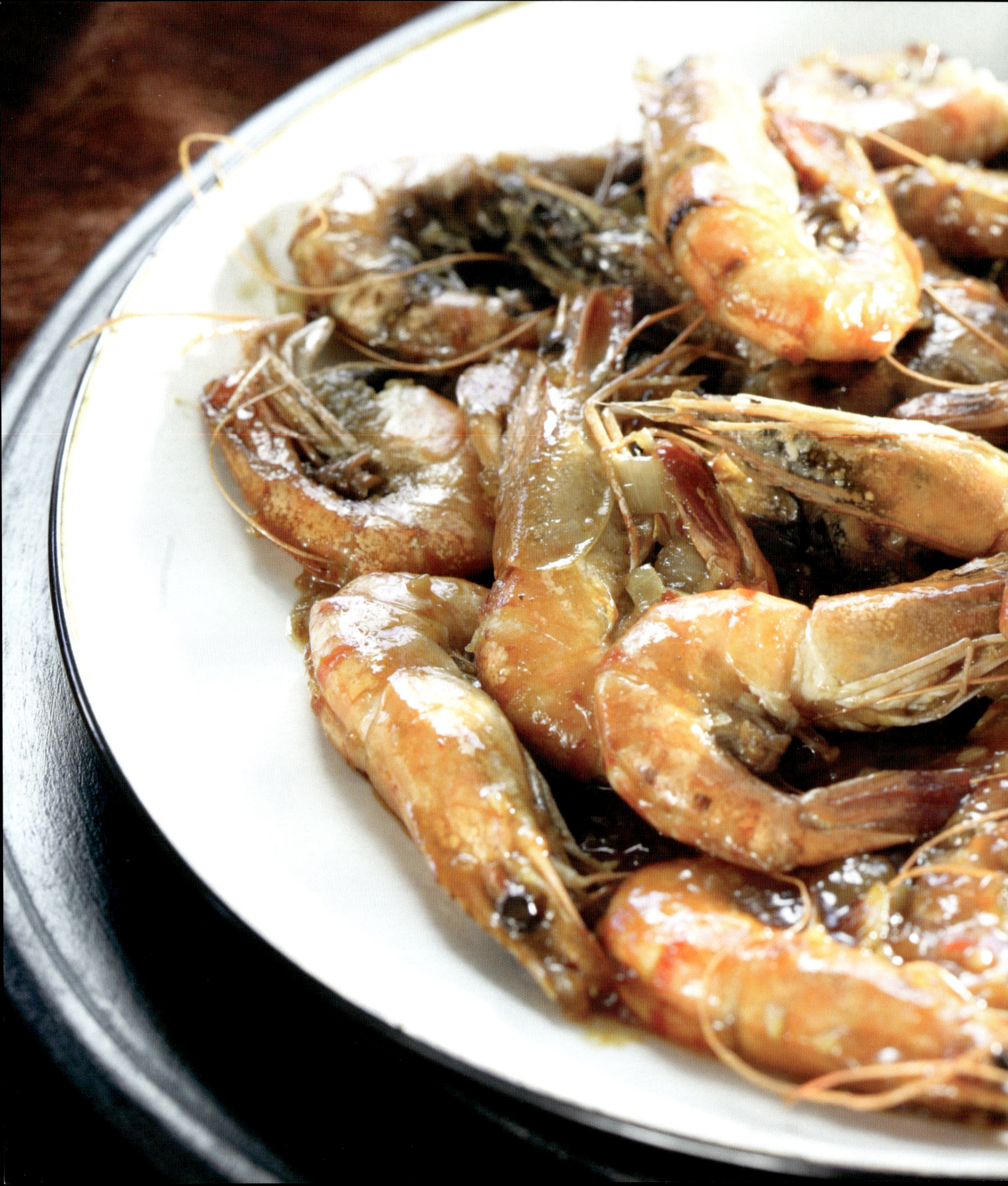

Peri Peri Prawns

It really is my own creation and stems from my penchant for all things hot and spicy. I made it as a starter at one of our dinners my husband and I were hosting. It was such a hit with our guests that word got around in our circle of friends and everyone started asking me to make them my Peri Peri Prawns. The dish is now known as "Prawns a la Bassie"!

Ingredients

800g	prawns in the shell
4	cloves fresh garlic, chopped
1	finger ginger, roughly grated
250g	unsalted butter
100ml	peri peri sauce or 15ml peri peri powder

Serves 4

Method

Heat a large frying pan or wok, and add the butter, garlic and ginger. Simmer to release the flavours.

Fry the prawns in batches in the butter. Once done, add all the prawns back into the pan or wok.

Add the peri peri sauce and serve with savoury rice.

Notes

Should you use the peri peri powder in this recipe, add the powder to the garlic and ginger.

Then fry in order for the powder to cook. There is nothing worse than the taste of raw spices!

Reg Zascaris

Advertising and Marketing Mogul, and Founding Director of Business Against Crime South Africa

He's known as South Africa's grand master of advertising, who describes his pet obsession as "selling South Africa". President of the Africa, Middle East and Mediterranean region of the TBWA global advertising group, and founding partner of TBWS Hunt Lascaris South Africa, Reg Lascaris is definitely proudly South African.

The marketing and advertising mogul has the Midas touch, putting this country firmly on the international map with TBWA Hunt Lascaris winning countless awards, notably named by the *Financial Mail* as Agency of the Century, and again recently as Agency of the Decade.

The African National Congress got Lascaris's agency on board to handle the first democratic election in South Africa. Then, four years later, the agency was again chosen to handle the election for Thabo Mbeki, who went on to become President.

Lascaris also worked with Cyril Ramaphosa on the communication of the development of the new Constitutuion, and Ramaphosa is today chairman of TBWA Hunt Lascaris.

As if that's not enough, Lascaris is also an accomplished author of five bestsellers, and a founding director of Business Against Crime South Africa.

You've got to love this guy who told the world that we have the biggest and best smiles around. "Nobody smiles like South Africans do," Lascaris famously said. "We're world champions at it because we're not afraid to practise in public."

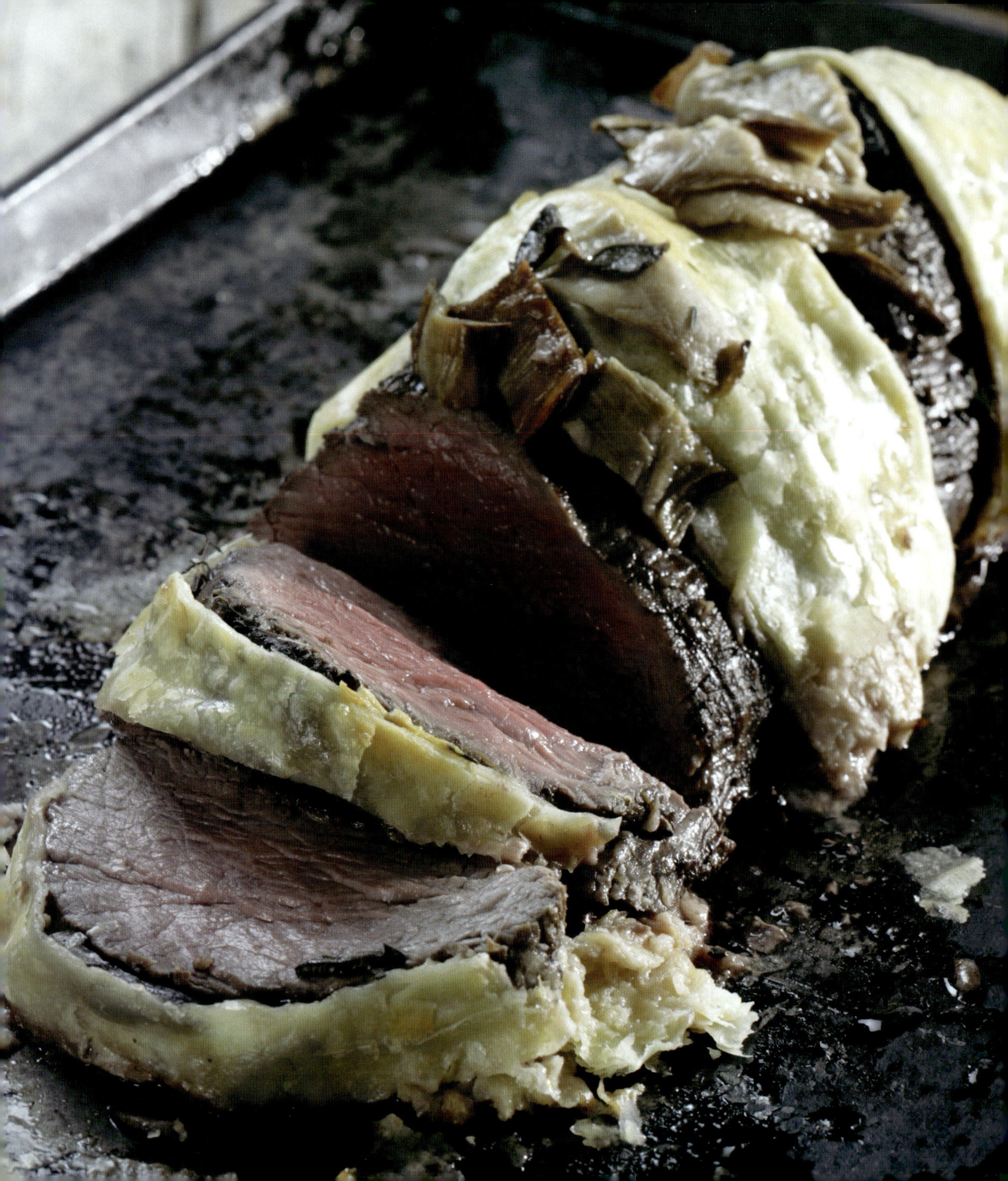

Fillet in Pastry

I'm not really a pudding man – except perhaps finishing a meal with a sorbet – but to me a simple, varied meal with a fresh salad is perfect. For this dish, a fresh, crisp lettuce and avocado, cucumber and spring onion salad with the juice of a lemon and some good olive oil is as close to perfection as it could get.

Ingredients

500g	whole fillet of beef
250g	mushrooms, sliced
	salt and freshly ground black pepper to taste
	few sprigs fresh rosemary
100ml	olive oil
60ml	flour
400g	frozen puff pastry, defrosted
1 egg	beaten
30ml	dijon mustard

Serves 4

Method

Preheat the oven to 180°C.

Trim all sinew off the fillet. Mix the salt and pepper and rub it into the meat.

Heat a frying pan, add the oil and seal the fillet on all sides. Remove from pan.

Add the mushrooms to the pan, turn down the heat and sauté for about 3 minutes. Remove from pan and set aside.

Sprinkle a board with the flour and roll out the puff pastry. Cut the pastry into strips of about 7cm wide.

Rub the rosemary and dijon mustard onto the meat, then pack the mushrooms around the meat.

Wrap the strips of pastry around the meat, wetting the ends so that it sticks together. Place the covered fillet on a smeared baking sheet. Brush the pastry with the beaten egg and place in the preheated oven.

Bake for 30–35 minutes. Remove from the oven and let the meat rest for about 5 minutes. Slice and serve with a salad.

Notes

Here is a tip: once you have rubbed the meat with the rosemary and mustard, place the strips of pastry on the smeared baking sheet, and place the fillet on top of the strips. Then pack the mushrooms onto the fillet, then finish wrapping the pastry around the meat, seal, brush with the egg and bake.

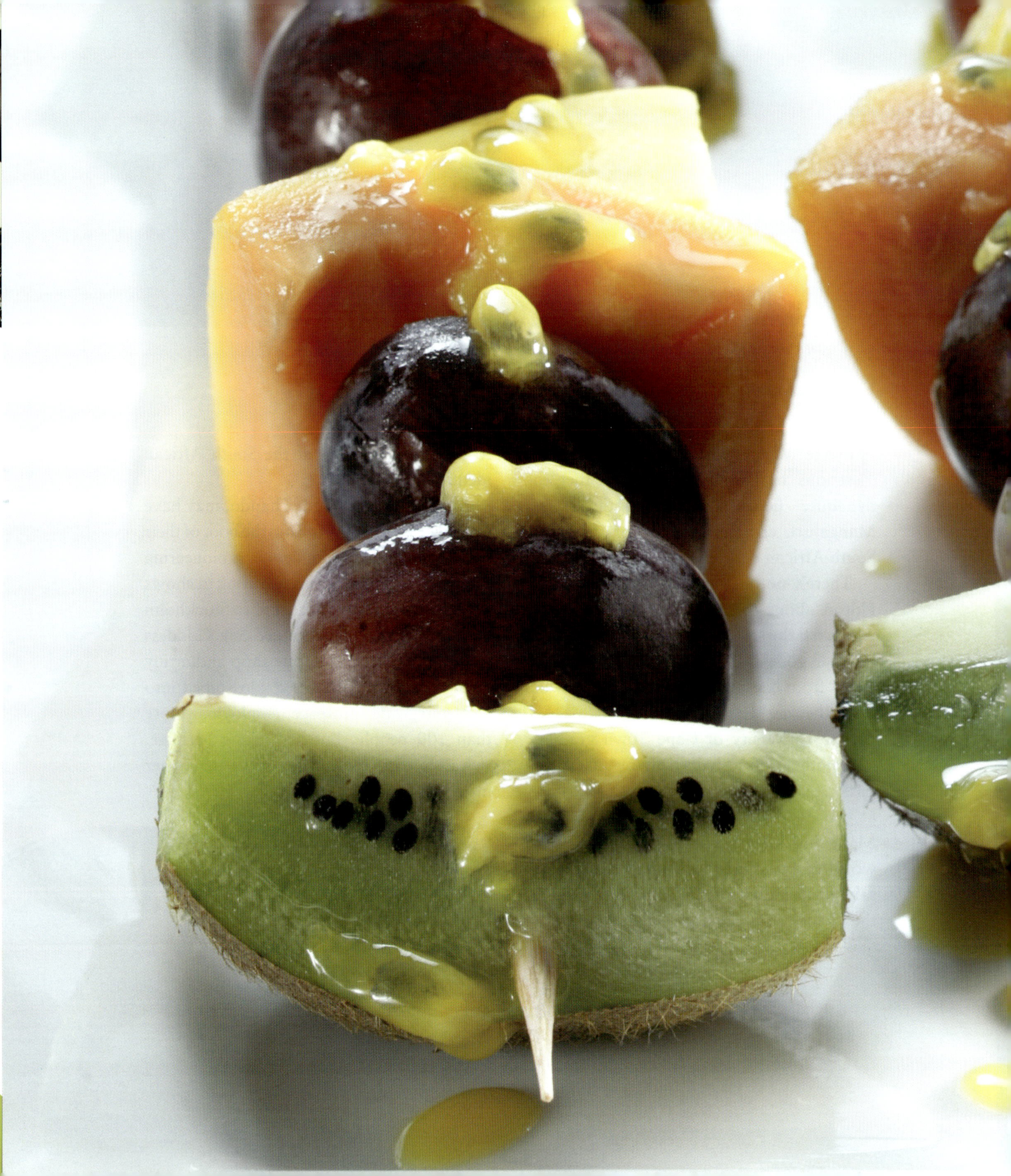

Tropical Fruit Kebabs

This dish is perfect for breakfast or a light dessert on a hot day. It is ideal for those who are watching their figures.

Ingredients

200g	paw paw
250g	kiwi fruit
200g	strawberries, halved
250g	white seedless grapes
125ml	granadilla pulp
4-6	wooden skewers

Serves 4-6

Method

Peel and cube the paw paw and kiwi fruit.

Thread alternate pieces of paw paw, kiwi fruit, strawberries and grapes onto the skewers and place on a serving dish.

Just before serving, drizzle the granadilla pulp over the skewers.

Dr Ivan R May

South African Marketing Doyen and Humanitarian

Described as "a true champion of the arts in South Africa" and someone who creates opportunities where none are to be found, Dr Ivan May is a true multi-dimensional man. Quiet and unassuming, May joined the banking fraternity after leaving his job as a biology lecturer to do an MBA, making that rare jump from trained academic to extraordinary success in the commercial world.

Currently chief executive of the Intellectual Capital Corporation of Africa and *1485am Radio Today*, a BBC World Service and Channel Africa partner, May has turned his hand, with unique success, to everything from the arts and radio, to wildlife and fundraising, most notably for the Children's Childhood Cancer Foundation (CHOC) in South Africa through the hugely successful *Cow Parade*. It was May who persuaded Nedbank to set up a Green Trust, and to orientate their entire corporate image and funding towards environmental issues. A doyen of marketing, May generously shares his wealth of experience in both the corporate and non-profit organisation sector, many of whom he has helped, voluntarily, to thrive and flourish.

Always in great demand as a speaker, lecturer and consultant, May is definitely the man to listen to when he says marketing is integral to the sustainability and very survival of organisations in today's competitive environment. He is a man whose life and work poignantly portray his belief that everything on this beautiful planet has as much of a right to be here as we do.

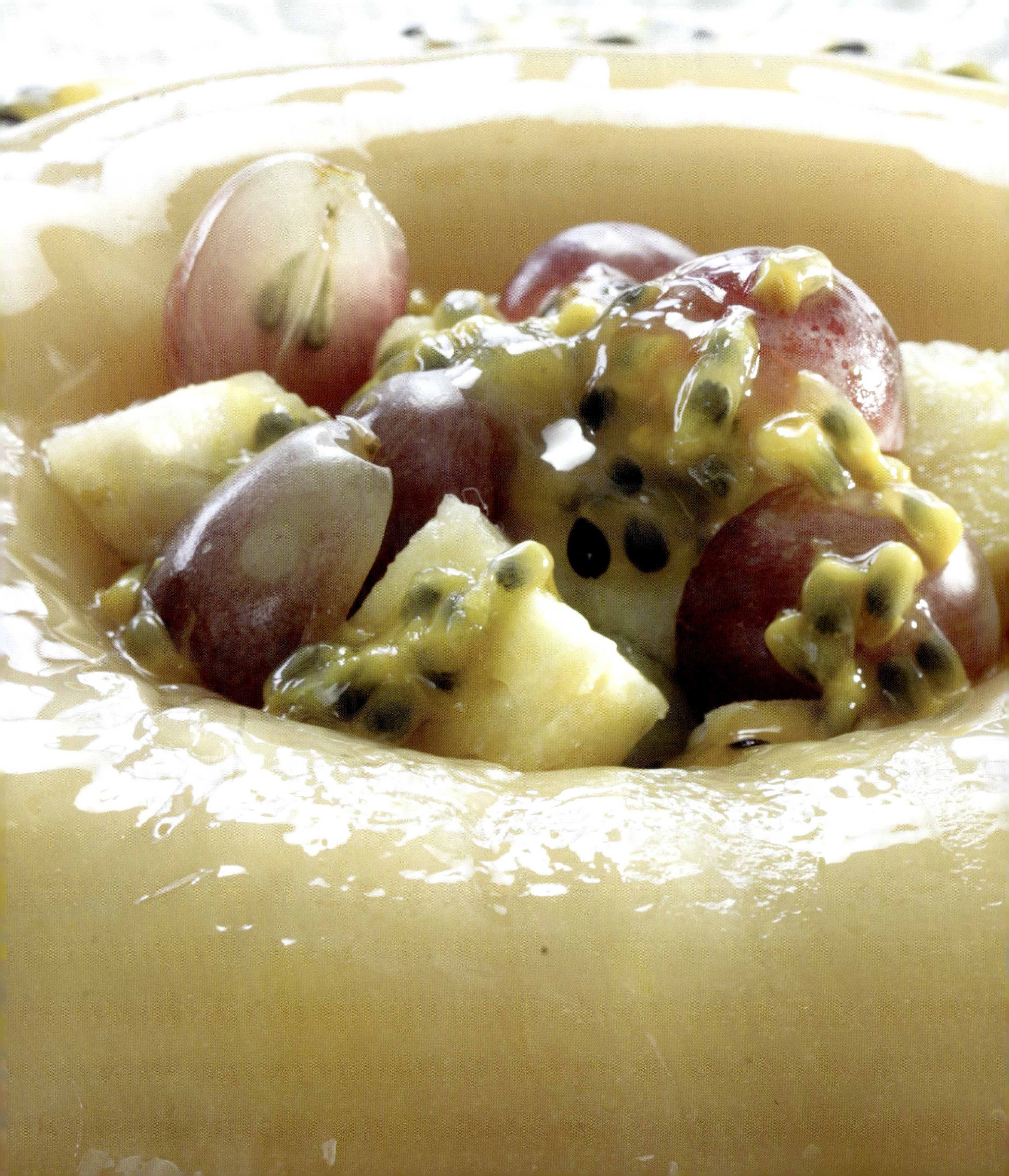

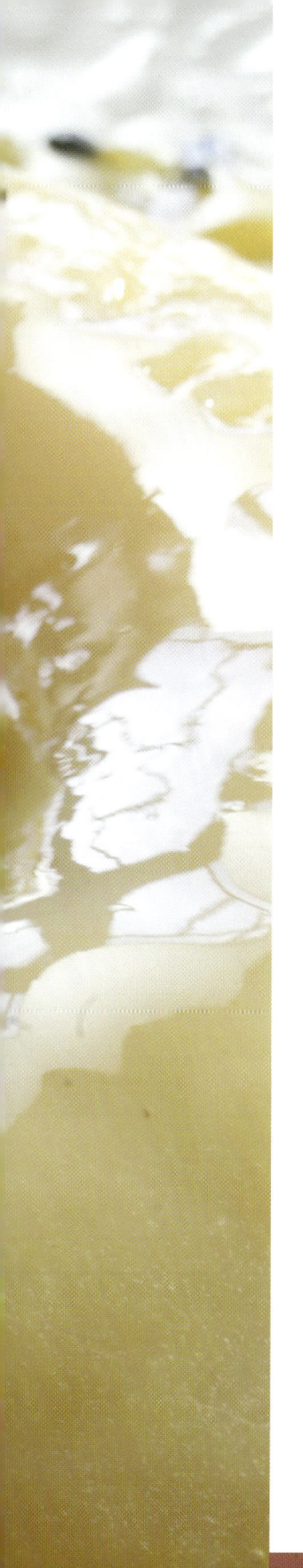

Ouma's Granadilla Pudding

I've chosen a really tried and tested recipe handed down from my grandmother and mother, so covering the Victorian, Edwardian (VII) and Georgian (VI) eras in South Africa. They have stuck in my mind as signature dishes, and their enjoyment remains profound, even in this new millennium.

Ingredients

250ml	sugar
600ml	boiling water
14-16	granadillas (2 tins)
10ml	maizena (cornflour)
2.5ml	lemon juice
2	egg whites

Serves 4-6

Method

Bring the sugar and water to the boil and stir until all the sugar has dissolved.

Meanwhile mix the granadilla pulp, maizena and lemon juice together to a thin creamy mixture.

Add the granadilla mixture to the boiling sugar water, and bring to the boil again stirring for 5 minutes.

Rub the mixture through a sieve. Leave to cool at room temperature.

Spray a ring mould with 'spray and cook'.

Whisk the two egg whites until soft peak stage and fold into the granadilla mixture. Pour into the mould and let set.

Turn the mould out onto a serving plate; decorate with fresh fruit, cream or maraschino cherries – whatever takes your fancy.

Notes

The texture should not be jelly-like. It must be soft and oh so silky to the taste – so go carefully on the maizena!

Ina Paarman

One of South Africa's Best-loved Foodies

Her name is familiar across South Africa for her range of sauces, cake mixes, pestos and stocks, as well as for her prolific output of cookery books. But Ina Paarman, one of the country's best-known and well-loved food writers and television personalities, has never forgotten how it all started out in a converted garage in Cape Town. Her "fairy tale" delivered in every way, with Paarman Foods today a respected, multi-million rand food company.

Paarman puts it all down to family: "I can't think of any other business unit that works as well as a tight family group. There is something very wholesome about a family business." And wholesome is the name of Paarman's game, whether it's between the pages of her many popular cookery books, or in her products which have become household names since she started out producing Seasoned Sea Salt, mixed up from grandmother Anna's recipe, in the 1980s.

In 1995, they started exporting their range of gourmet sauces and seasonings, and in 1998 broke into the local food service arena, supplying customised products to restaurants and franchised food groups.

Paarman says she's obsessive about quality and authenticity, and that passion is the prime motivator for her success. And plenty of South Africans thank her for that!

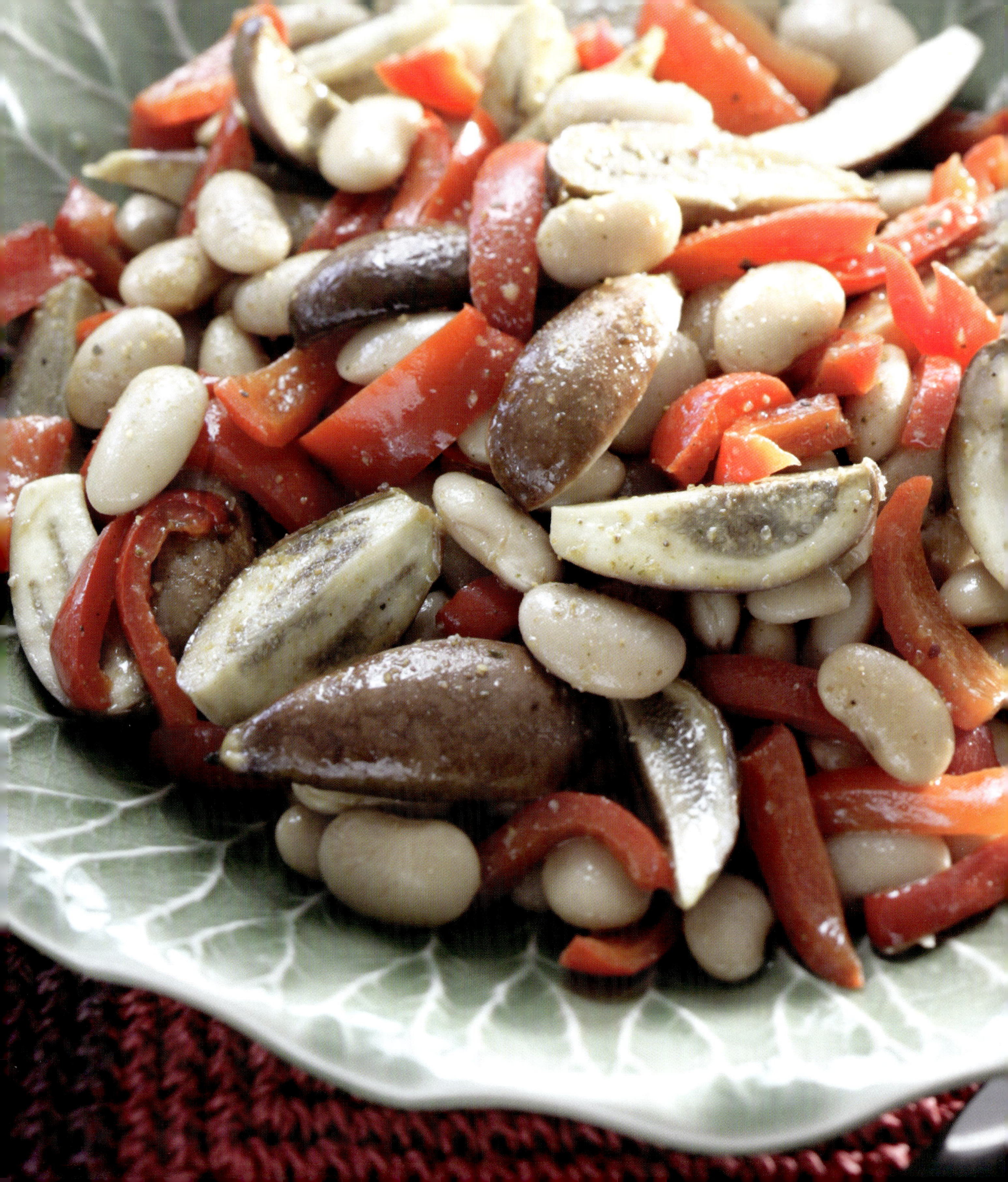

Butter Bean and Roast Vegetable Salad

I selected this recipe because after we tested and perfected it here in our test kitchen, I tried it on my weekend guests and then used it on our Website as one of our regular Menu of the Month features. Rave reviews all round!

Ingredients

1 tin	(1x400g) butter beans, well drained (one of my regular store-cupboard basics!)
2	medium aubergines (eggplants), unpeeled and cubed 1cm x 2cm
2	red bell peppers, deseeded and cut into strips
125ml	Ina Paarman's Greek Lemon vinaigrette
10ml	Ina Paarman's Reduced Salt Garlic & Herb seasoning
	Ina Paarman's Chilli and Garlic Seasoning

Serves 4-6

Method

Preheat the oven to 200°C.

Toss the vegetables in an oven roasting pan with the vinaigrette dressing and seasoning. Shake the pan to level out the vegetables to an even layer.

Roast, open, for 40 minutes until the aubergines are soft and the peppers slightly charred.

Toss with the butter beans, season to taste with the chilli & garlic seasoning and dish into a serving dish.

Serve slightly warm or at room temperature.

Aviva Pelham

Popular Opera Diva

Aviva Pelham is the woman with the voice described as a "superb instrument", a vivacious soprano who attracts capacity audiences and then holds them captive with her astonishing charisma. But if it is true that a singer worthy of the label "artiste" must have artistic integrity and passion, there's no arguing that Pelham has more than earned her stripes.

Dynamic and versatile whether she's doing opera, operetta, musicals or cabaret, the petite soprano is committed to community projects and is regularly seen on stage introducing exceptionally gifted singers she's discovered in disadvantaged communities, and for whom she seeks funding and mentors. This is the result of workshops she gives regularly in township areas, working closely with young singers. But Pelham also trains the choir at Pollsmoor Prison, as well as the Monkeybiz Aids Choir. She says she's committed herself to making a difference through her work, and uses her expertise and experience to help with a wide range of programmes, lectures, demonstrations, concerts and workshops.

"It's imperative to take music projects to the schools so that young, classically trained singers can become role-models to new generations of children and to provide a platform for gifted young singers from previously disadvantaged communities. It's such a huge privilege working with such talent", is how Pelham explains her passion. It's a long way from the stages of London, Israel and Paris, and from singing for the Queen and Nelson Mandela, but Pelham wouldn't have it any other way.

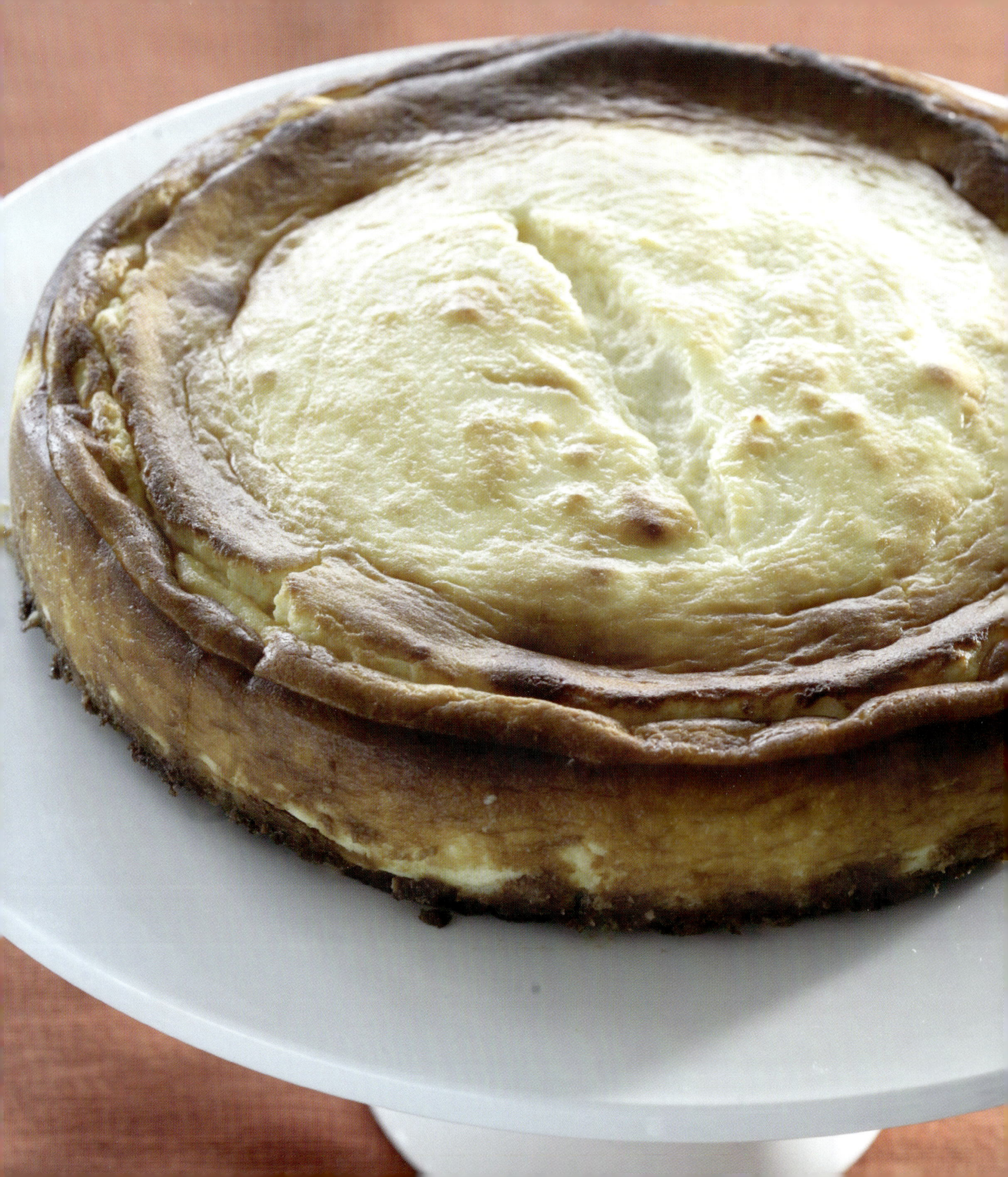

Warm Fluffy Baked Cheesecake

This totally meltingly comfortingly and overwhelmingly delicious cheesecake can be used as a dessert or for tea-time... but always, remember to serve it warm.

Ingredients

1	packet marie biscuits
125g	butter (soft)
2	eggs
125ml	sugar
15ml	custard powder
400g	plain cream cheese
5ml	vanilla
1ml	lemon juice
150ml	cream

Serves 4-6

Method

Pre-heat oven to 180°C.

Crumble biscuits and add soft butter to make a crumbly paste.

Line a buttered oven dish, but save a little to sprinkle on the top of the cake.

Mix 2 egg yolks with 125ml sugar. Add the custard powder.

Then add the cream cheese, vanilla and lemon juice.

Beat the egg whites until soft peaks form, and fold in.

Beat the cream until it starts to thicken and add in gently.

Pour the mixture into the lined oven dish and bake for half an hour.

Serve warm.

Francois Pienaar

Former Springbok Rugby Captain turned Banker

Who could forget Francois Pienaar's centre-stage role in that defining "Rainbow Nation" moment when Nelson Mandela donned a rugby jersey bearing the Springbok captain's number, to congratulate him on South Africa's famous 1995 Rugby World Cup win.

It was the ultimate prize for a rugby match unlike any the Springboks had played before, with South Africans of all races and religions coming together for an unprecedented celebration.

Pienaar was acknowledged as an inspiring leader, with an uncompromising approach to commitment. So his list of accolades is hardly surprising – South African Rugby Player of the Year in 1993, International Rugby Player of the Year in 1994, International Rugby Captain of the Year in 1995, and Rugby Personality of the Year in 1996 (nominated by the top 20 rugby writers in Britain). In 2004 he was also voted into 50th spot on the list of 100 Great South Africans.

Today Pienaar is the Provincial Chairman of First National Bank in the Western Cape, but that moment when he became an official part of South Africa's democratic history is permanently etched in his memory. Pienaar recalls: "What happened was Nelson Mandela said 'thank you very much for what you've done for South Africa', but I said 'thank *you* for what you've done'. I almost felt like hugging him, but it wasn't appropriate, I guess."

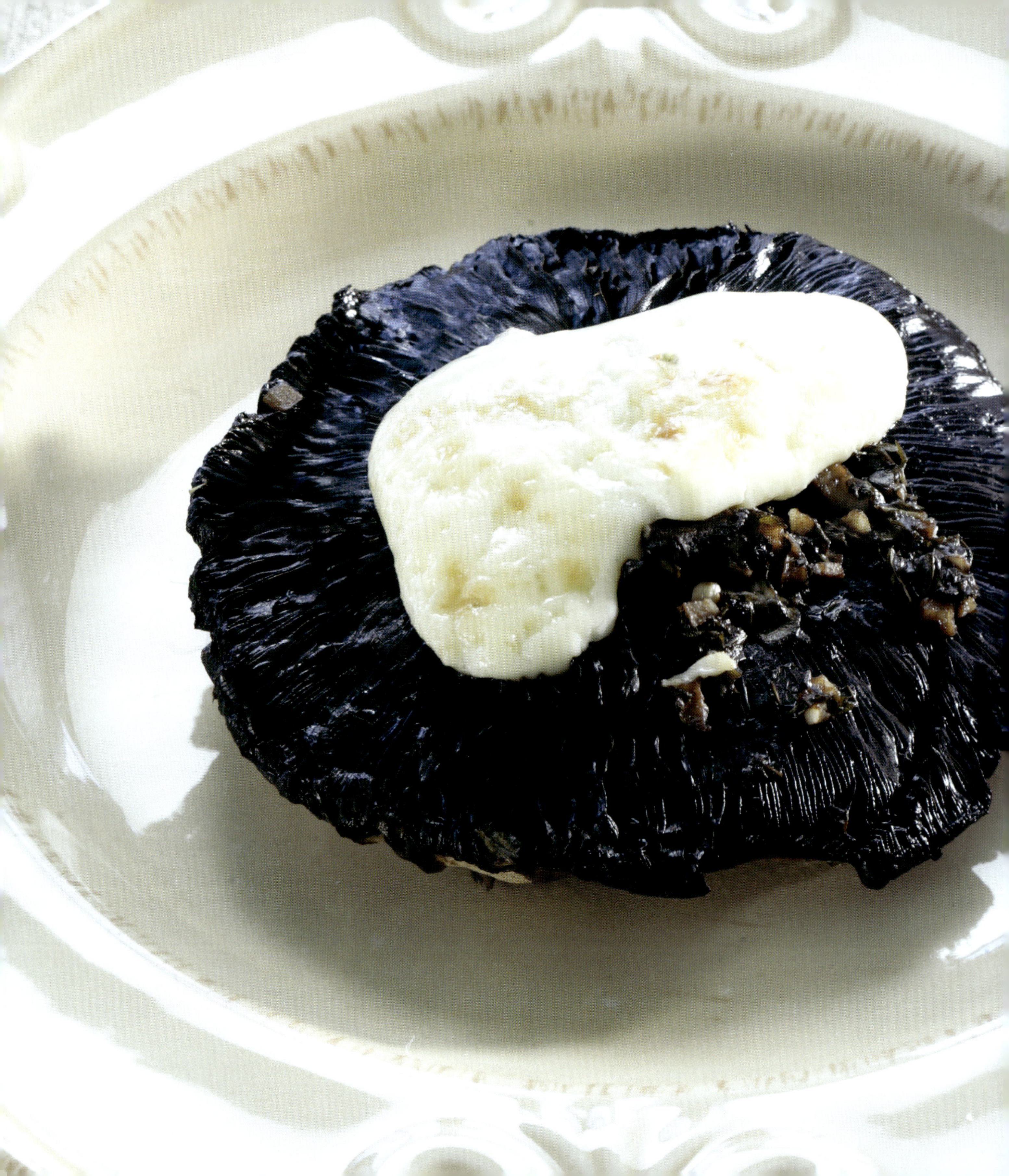

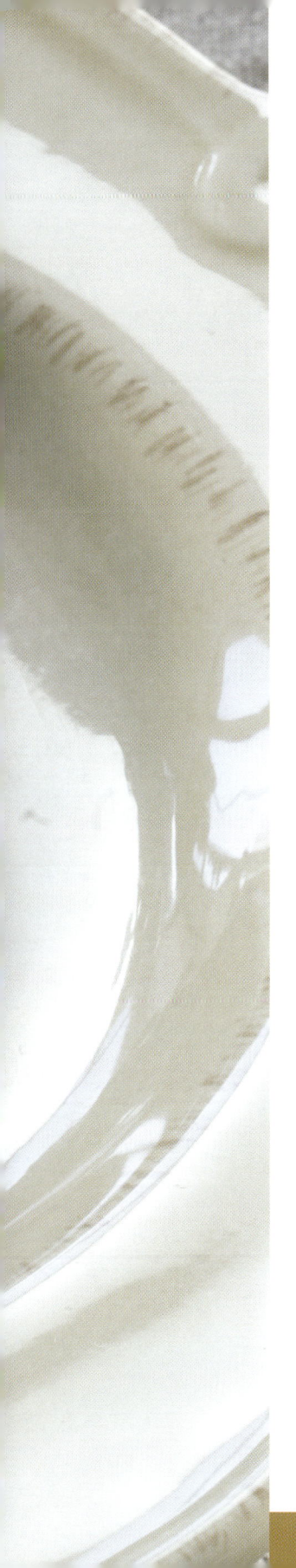

Grilled Herb-marinated Portabella Mushrooms with Gorgonzola

This is ideal as a starter for a dinner party or a braai – especially if that fire takes a bit too long to form coals. It will line the stomach and you will not die of starvation.

Ingredients

8	large portabella or brown mushrooms
3	cloves garlic, finely chopped*
10	fresh mint leaves, chopped*
15	fresh basil leaves, torn*
5ml	fresh oregano, chopped*
15ml	parsley, chopped*
	black pepper to taste*
30ml	red wine vinegar*
60ml	balsamic vinegar*
125ml	extra virgin olive oil*
180g	gorgonzola cheese, cut into chunks
	radicchio or rocket leaves to serve

Serves 4

Method

Wipe the mushrooms with a damp cloth – do not wash, as they will absorb water. Using a sharp utility knife, score a criss-cross pattern lightly into the top of the mushroom. This will help it absorb more of the marinade. Place into a shallow dish or sealed zip-lock bag.

Place all remaining ingredients marked with * into a spill-proof container. Shake vigorously and pour over mushrooms.

Let marinate for 30 minutes to 1 hour. Do not let sit for too long or they will become soggy. Turn mushrooms over to marinate on both sides. Do not put in refrigerator.

Grill the mushrooms over a hot barbeque grill or under an oven grill until brown on each side.

When almost finished, turn the mushroom on its back, stem facing upwards, place a couple of pieces of the cheese on each mushroom and place under the grill again until it is melted.

Serve on top of radicchio or rocket leaves.

Gary Player

Golfing Legend

His penchant for wearing black outfits on the golf course, combined with his fiercely competitive nature, gave golfing legend Gary Player the name by which he is known worldwide – The Black Knight. But there's nothing dark about the heart of this "legend in his own time", regarded as one of the greatest players in the history of the game.

Through the efforts of The Player Foundation, he has raised more than R100 million globally for education for underprivileged children, spurred on by memories of the three-hour roundtrip to school he walked daily as a boy. And no one would expect anything less from the man who turned professional at just 17, joined the PGA Tour four years later, and who to date has notched up top honours in 163 professional golf tournaments worldwide, including nine major championships on the regular tour and nine majors on the champions tour. Most significantly, he is one of only five players ever to win the career Grand Slam.

Recognised internationally as an uncompromising perfectionist who settles for nothing but the best, Player's philosophy extends to his own stringent health and fitness regimen which also earned him the title, Mr Fitness. And that's got to be an essential, considering he's also considered the World's Most Travelled Athlete – with more than 14 million miles logged… and still counting.

Whether it's in business with his son Marc through Black Knight International, on the race track where he breeds fine thoroughbred race horses, or in the architect game where Player is credited with the design of over 250 championship golf courses, this is definitely a man with the Midas touch. Courageous and competitive, but always courteous, Gary Player is known as a true gentleman.

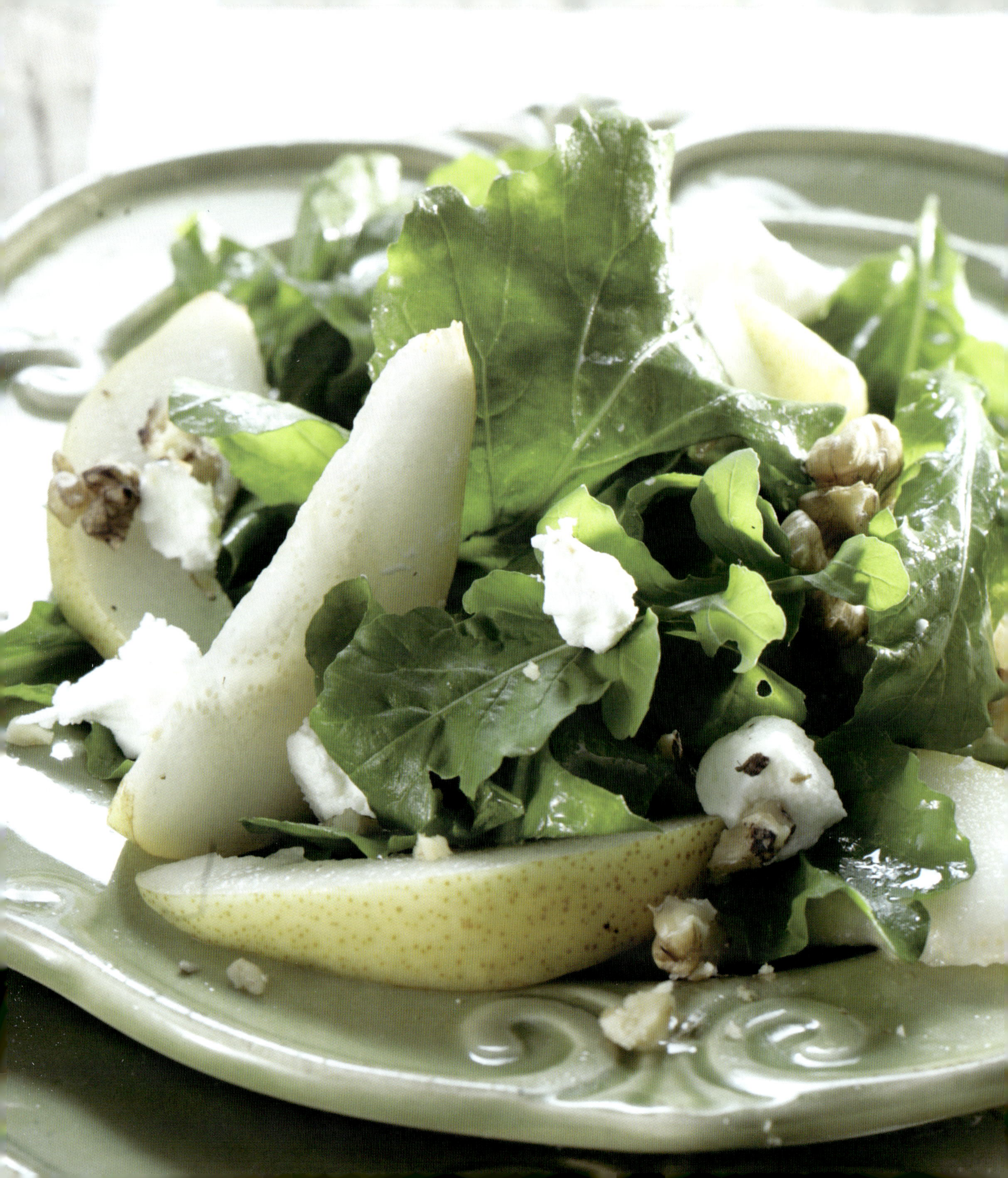

Pear and Goat's Cheese with Rocket and Lemon Oil

The peppery taste of the rocket with the zing of the lemon oil blends perfectly with the pears and the soft creamy texture of the cheese.

Ingredients

2	ripe packham of forelle pears
150g	soft goat's cheese
100g	rocket leaves
60ml	toasted walnuts
	olive oil for dressing the leaves
1	lemon

Serves 4

Method

Slice the pear as thinly as possible, cutting towards the core and stopping before you reach the seeds. Discard the core. Zest the lemon over the pears and set aside.

Slice the goat's cheese into thin discs or small squares and set aside.

To finish, pick and wash the rocket leaves and dry thoroughly in a salad spinner. Place in a mixing bowl and cover with just enough oil to barely coat the leaves. You should need about 15ml.

Squeeze the juice from the lemon over the rocket. Toss the rocket so the lemon and oil coat the leaves thoroughly all over.

In serving bowls, start layering up the leaves, goat's cheese, walnuts and pears, seasoning with sea salt and fresh black pepper as you go.

Gavin Rajah

Fashion and Marketing Maestro

"Unashamedly opulent and ultra-feminine, the designs of South African fashion maestro Gavin Rajah won't do for the 'wallflower' woman. They are for confident and assertive women who exude femininity – like Beyonce, Jodie Kidd, Tina Turner and Cameron Diaz, all celebrities who have fallen under the Rajah spell.

But for all the fortune and fame he's won both nationally and around the world, Rajah's heart is with the less fortunate for whom he works tirelessly. He's passionate about working for charity, and in 2006 launched POSITIVE, a personal initiative to raise funds for children with HIV/Aids in South Africa. The event, sponsored and adopted by Sun International, was the first Pan-African collaboration featuring designers, artists and musicians in one singular performance headlined by international artist Seal.

That same year he made South African history when he was invited by the Federation Francaise de la Couture to show his couture collection in Paris. Rajah has also turned his hand to helping empower destitute and unemployed South Africans, teaching them traditional skills like beading, embroidery, jewellery component manufacture, and tailoring. And he's passionately promoting these projects to the rest of the world – in between being a judge for Holland's Next Top Model, and launching a jewellery collection in Japan.

Rajah has recently been appointed UNICEF Goodwill Ambassador, recognising his transformative contributions to the lives of South African children and their families.

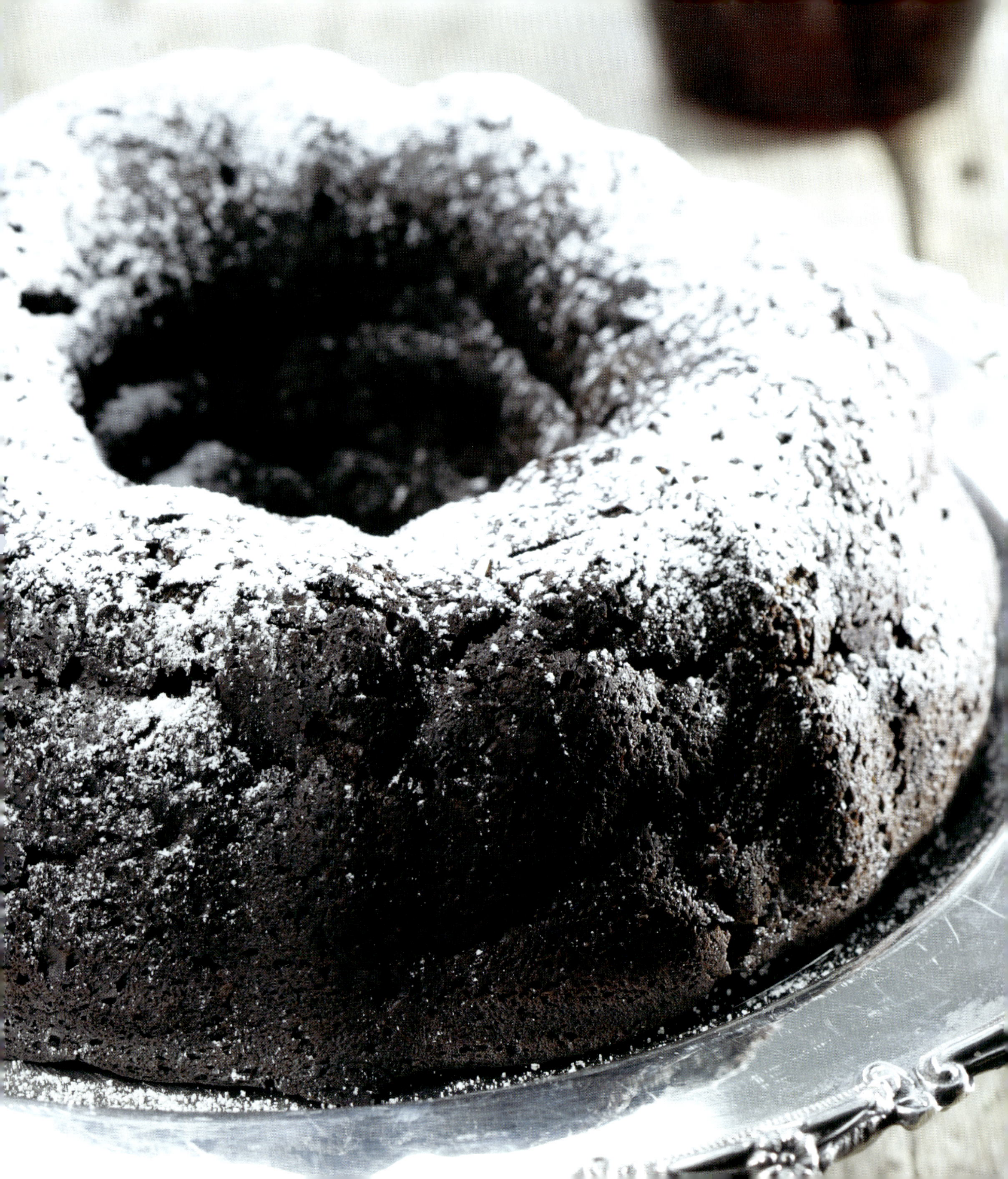

The Raj's Decadent Chocolate Cake

This is chocolate, chocolate, chocolate. This cake is so rich, there's absolutely no need for frosting.

Ingredients

500ml	sour cream
3	eggs
85ml	sunflower oil
125ml	coffee-flavoured liqueur
500ml	chopped albany or dark chocolate
1	package dark chocolate cake mix
1	package instant chocolate pudding mix

Serves 6-8

Method

Preheat the oven to 175°C.

Grease and flour a 25cm bundt pan (the one with the hole in the centre).

In a large bowl, combine the cake mix, pudding mix, sour cream, eggs, oil and coffee liqueur.

Beat until ingredients are well blended.

Fold in the chopped chocolate pieces – the batter will be thick.

Spoon the batter into the prepared pan.

Bake in preheated oven for 1 hour, or until cake springs back when lightly pressed.

Notes

Cool on a wire rack and turn… then be prepared to impress your friends!

Jane Raphaely

Chairperson of Associated Magazines

Magazine mogul, Jane Raphaely, showed men that a woman's place is definitely at the helm of big business long before the new South Africa afforded her gender an equal spot in the limelight.

The year was 1965 and Raphaely, today a leading publisher of quality magazines in southern Africa and a household name among generations of loyal magazine afficionados, founded *Fair Lady* for Nasionale Pers. That was just the first step on her ladder to success, and 18 years later, in 1983, she set up the company that proudly bears her name, Jane Raphaely and Associates – and women got a second choice of a quality magazine designed specifically for them, *Cosmopolitan*.

In 1988, Associated Magazines was born, and published *Femina*. *Brides and Homes* followed in 1998, and in 1993, *House and Leisure* entered the market on a monthly basis. *Marie Claire* was added to the stable in 2003. Associated Magazines is also the only publisher outside the US to publish O, The Oprah Magazine.

Raphaely was a woman before her time, and thanks to her vision has played a pivotal role in publishing for women in South Africa. In 2007, Associated Magazines, reached more than 1.5 million readers every month. And there is little doubt that her company's mentoring and empowering role in publishing since 1983 is what's to thank for many of the most influential journalists practising their craft in South Africa today.

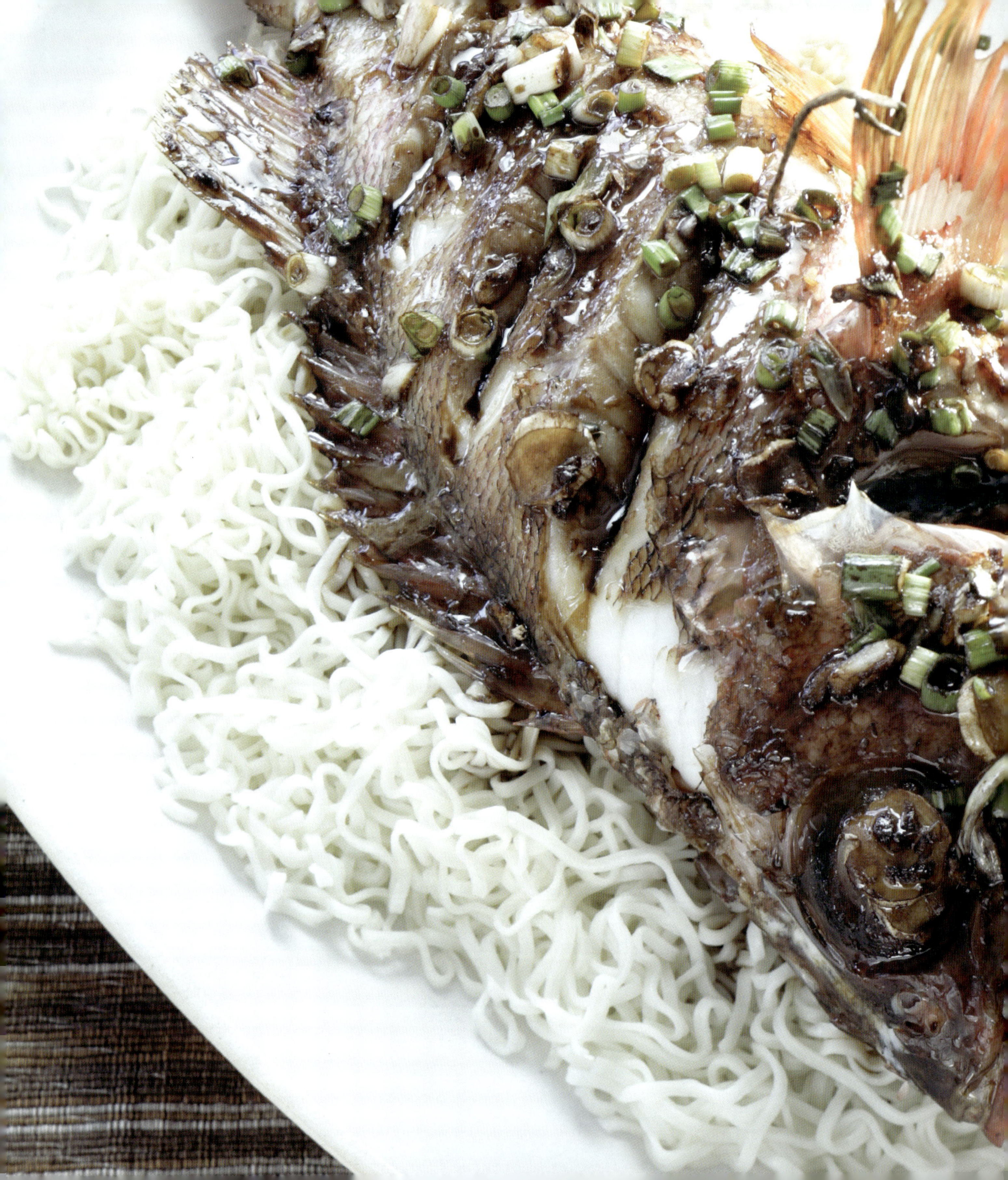

Whole Roasted Chinese Fish

I love Chinese food and much of it is surprisingly easy to do because it is so quick and simple. Everything is in the ingredients. It looks magnificent on a large blue and white antique china platter, if you are lucky enough to have one. Let people help themselves. That's part of the fun. Serve with buckwheat noodles and the long-stemmed broccoli. Both go well with the soy and spring onion sauce. Today it is increasingly difficult to source kabeljou, even in Cape Town where the sea is still full of them. We are competing with other countries and very often the weather makes things even worse. Cape salmon would be my second choice, since stumpnose and musselcracker are even more difficult to source legally.

Ingredients

1	whole kabeljou (approx. weight 3.5kg)
125ml	soy sauce
1	bunch spring onion, chopped
1	clove of garlic, crushed
30ml	olive oil
	juice of one lemon
	salt to taste
	generous amount of ground black pepper

Serves 8-10

Method

Preheat the oven to 180°C. Line a baking tray with tin foil big enough for the fish.

Make incisions diagonally across the body of the fish.

Mix the soy sauce, lemon juice, chopped spring onion, crushed garlic and olive oil. Pour over the fish and marinate in the refrigerator for one hour before cooking.

Remove the fish from marinade and place on the lined baking tray.

Drizzle the remaining marinade over the fish and bake in the preheated oven for 45 minutes. The cooking time can vary, depending on the size of the fish.

Serve the fish with stir-fried vegetables or a green salad.

Notes

Kabeljou is the best fish for this recipe. If your time it right – 45 minutes at 180° for 4kg fish without the head – it will be succulent and tender. You must use lots of Kikkoman low sodium soy sauce, stuff the fish lavishly with whole spring onions and cook it on a bed of them too.

Zannice Snyman

Culinary Guru, Author and Publisher

'She's been described as smart – but with a tongue sharp as a chef's knife. She's one of South Africa's most experienced and well-respected food personalities, whose contribution to the country's culinary scene has been hailed as "invaluable". She's Lannice Snyman, contemporary culinary writer, consultant and publisher extraordinaire, and southern Africa's Academy Head for The World's 50 Best Restaurants organised by *Restaurant magazine* in London.

Foodie, fundi or culinary guru – call her what you will, but it is the achievements of the woman who in 2006 got a Lifetime Achievement Award for her contribution to South Africa's culinary scene that speak for themselves. Author of 15 books that have sold around half a million copies, Snyman has notched up several national and international awards, but is especially known as founder editor of *Eat Out* restaurant guide, which she headed for 18 years.

It's hardly surprising then that she's lauded for doing so much, not only for recording and documenting South Africa's cuisine, but also for making it accessible. South Africa is proud of its good food traditions, and putting back the fun into local food is a skill that Snyman has perfected.

If countries are defined by their cuisine, then Snyman must certainly be defined by not only her expertise, but also her charm, warmth, humour, and a healthy dose of eccentricity.

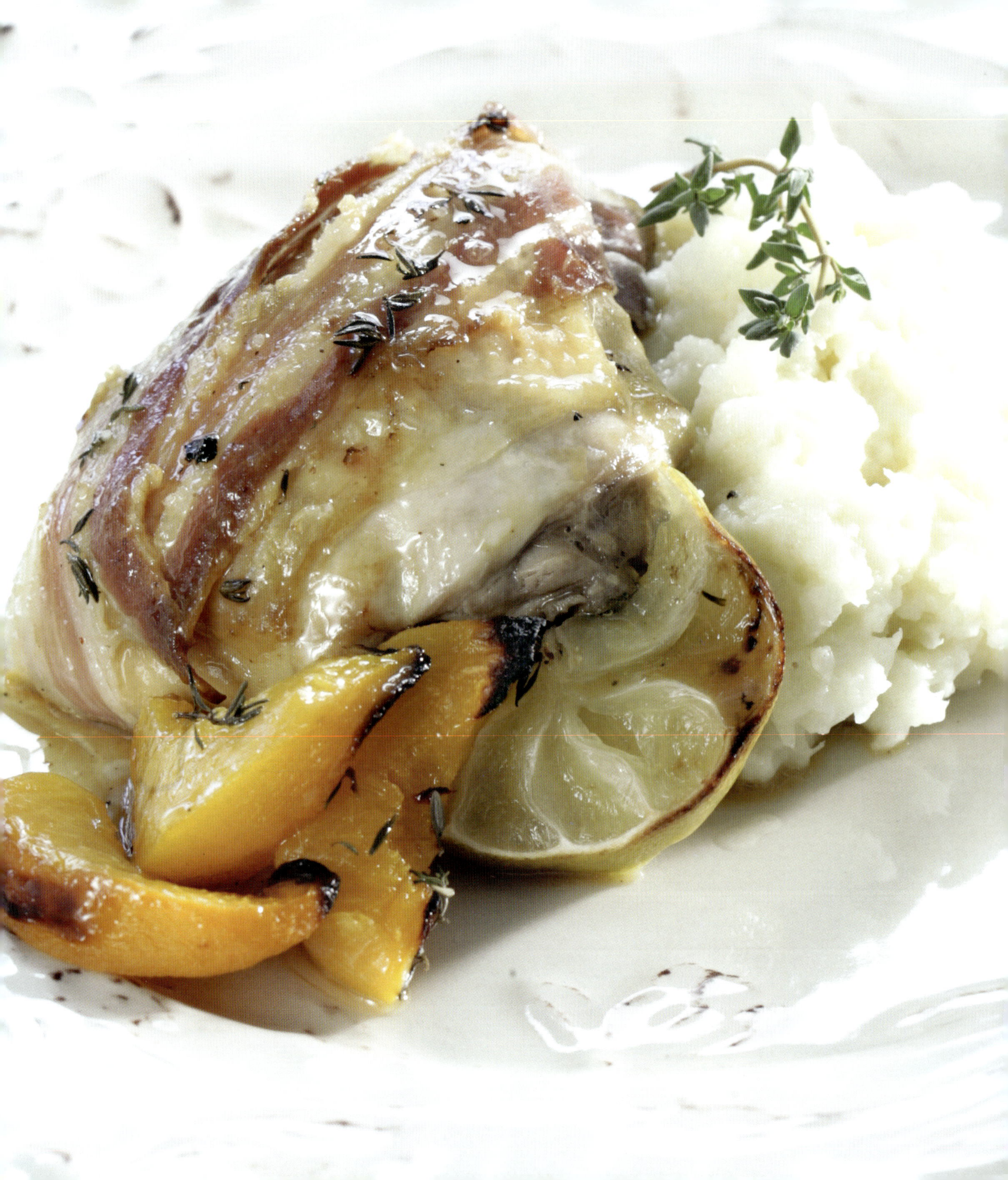

Chicken with Peaches and Pancetta on Mashed Cauliflower

I (unashamedly) wove my favourite ingredients into short, sharp, smart recipes that could stand alone or be served together, depending on the whim of the reader.

Ingredients

8	free-range chicken thighs, skinned and boned
8	slices pancetta
1	lime, thinly sliced
1	clingstone peach, peeled, stoned and sliced
	butter
	leaves stripped from a small bunch thyme
	salt and milled black pepper

Mashed Cauliflower

500g	cauliflower, roughly chopped
500ml	milk
125ml	cream
	salt and milled black pepper
	grated nutmeg

Serves 4

Method

Preheat oven to 180°C.

Wrap each chicken thigh in a slice of pancetta.

Generously butter a baking dish large enough to accommodate all the ingredients. Add the lime slices and top with the chicken.

Scatter the peach slices and thyme all about and season lightly with salt and pepper.

Bake uncovered for about 35 minutes until the chicken is cooked, the pancetta crisp and the peaches gloriously tender and golden.

Mashed Cauliflower

Put the cauliflower into a medium saucepan with the milk and cream, and a pinch of salt, pepper and nutmeg.

Simmer gently uncovered for about 15 minutes until the cauliflower is very soft and the liquid has reduced by half. Drain the cauliflower; reserve the liquid.

Measure 150ml of the liquid; pour into a food processor with the cauliflower. Whiz fairly smoothly, adding more liquid if necessary. Return to the saucepan and reheat.

To serve, spoon mashed cauliflower onto warm plates and top with chicken, peaches and the pan-juices.

Notes

At a pinch, rindless streaky bacon could be used instead of pancetta.

And mangoes and nectarines are delicious in this recipe if peaches aren't about.

Peter Soldatos

Internationally Renowned Couturier

Plenty of South Africa's most elegant women already bow to the brilliance of top South African couturier Peter Soldatos, who breathes style while others make do with oxygen. He's dressed international stars like Nana Mouskouri, Liza Minnelli and even the late Liberace, during his decades-long reign in the South African fashion world where his judgment still leads. Soldatos' fashion collections have been greeted with acclaim in North America, Europe and Africa.

Ever outspoken, in 2001, when President Thabo Mbeki's wife Zanele took London's fashion world by storm, Soldatos gave her a definite vote of approval. Then he added the final barb: "She can teach the Queen a thing or two." But then Soldatos has always been very definite on the question of what makes women stylish.

Following the death in October last year of one of his former models from the 1970s, Port Elizabeth style icon Ivan Ofsowitz, he made it clear that "style is something you cannot differentiate, but you know it when you see it".

Soldatos believes "a woman should dress according to the life she leads, and the man she loves, and the size of her purse". So there you have it.

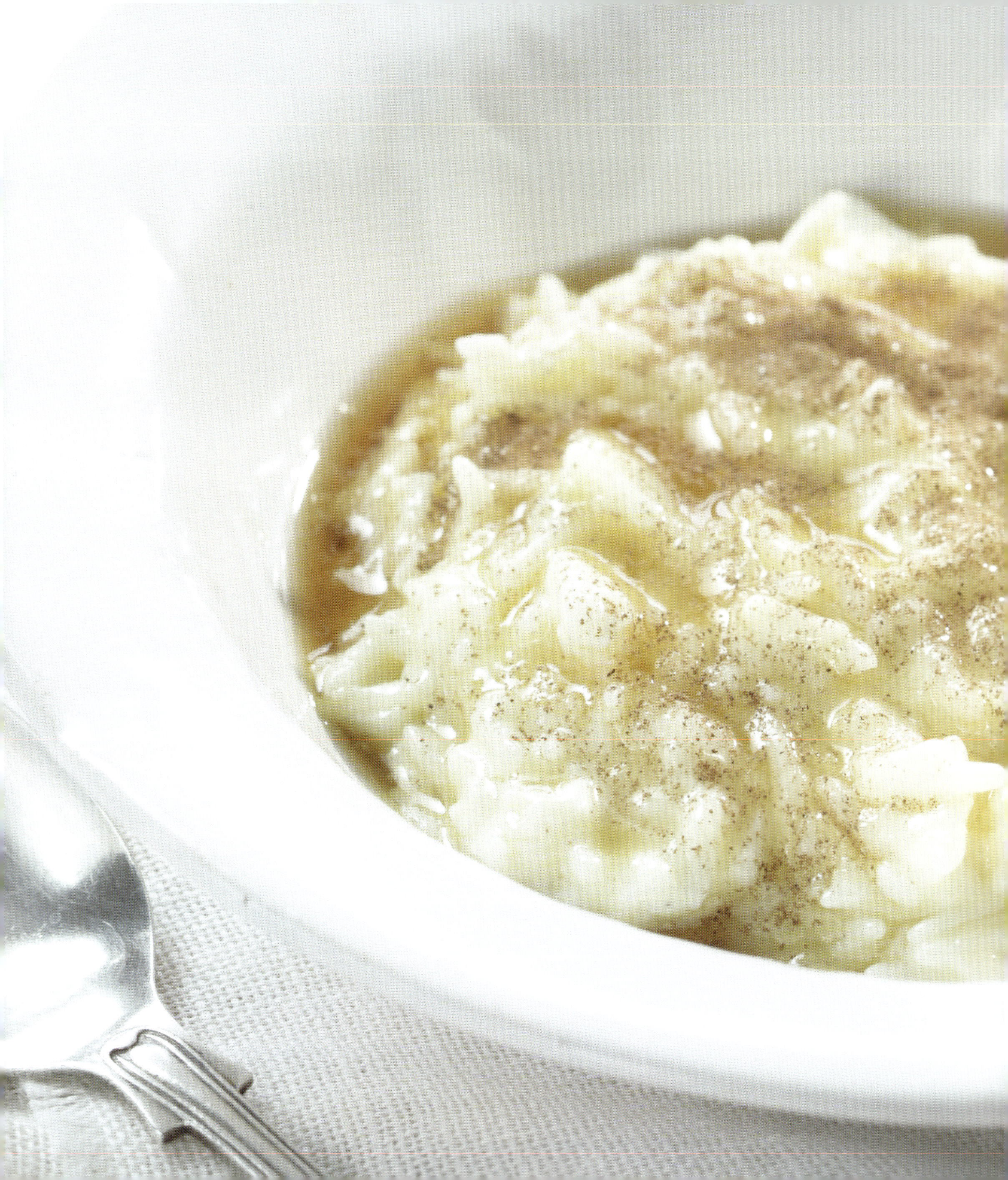

Rice Pudding

This is an old family recipe brought over from Greece by my ancestors. Like the Greek people, it is hardworking, quick and honest.

Ingredients

250ml	water
125ml	long grain rice
1 litre	milk
	rind of one orange (without the pith)
	pinch of salt
10ml	cornflour mixed into a paste with water
2	egg yolks
45ml	sugar
2.5ml	vanilla essence
	ground cinnamon

Serves 4

Method

In a thick-based saucepan bring the water to the boil, stir in the rice and cook gently until the water has absorbed.

Add the milk, orange rind and salt and bring to the boil stirring occasionally. Simmer over a low heat, uncovered until the rice is very tender.

Add the cornflour mixture while stirring continuously until the mixture thickens.

Whisk the egg yolks and sugar together in a bowl and add the mixture slowly to the rice while stirring for a few seconds.

Remove the saucepan from the heat; add the vanilla and dish into serving bowls. Sprinkle with cinnamon and serve.

Notes

This pudding can be served either hot or chilled.

Beyers Truter

World-acclaimed Pinotage King

Known around the world as the Pinotage King, and with red wine his undoubted passion, Beyers Truter is also a winemaker with a conscience. He has received the Robert Mondave Trophy for the best winemaker in the world, the Pichon Lonqueville Comtesse De La Lande Trophy for the best Blend Red (twice), the Warren Wanarski for the best Cabernet Sauvignon and made eight Pinotages that received the ABSA Top 10 Award. And this winemaker is also the driving force behind a movement to tackle Foetal Alcohol Syndrome, one of the most serious issues in the Western Cape Winelands. His Faith Fund (Foetal Alcohol Syndrome and Inter-related Treatment Help Fund) raises funds and distributes donations to specific projects, charities and other organisations working with children, families and communities affected by alcohol abuse.

The co-owner and winemaker of Beyerskloof remains adamant that his success is due "to the grace of God", so working to save children from preventable mental retardation is his way of giving back.

His list of local and international awards bears testament to his brilliance; like the famous Beyerskloof Pinotage, the estate's remarkable range of Pinotage-based reds are still fermented in old-fashioned open tanks. Beyerskloof was also one of the first Cape wines to enjoy early maturation in 100% new Nevers oak barriques for 24 months, and French oak still plays an important part in the ageing process.

He's come a long way since his arrival on the farm when he says he was met with "nothing but a donkey – oh ja, and some ducks".

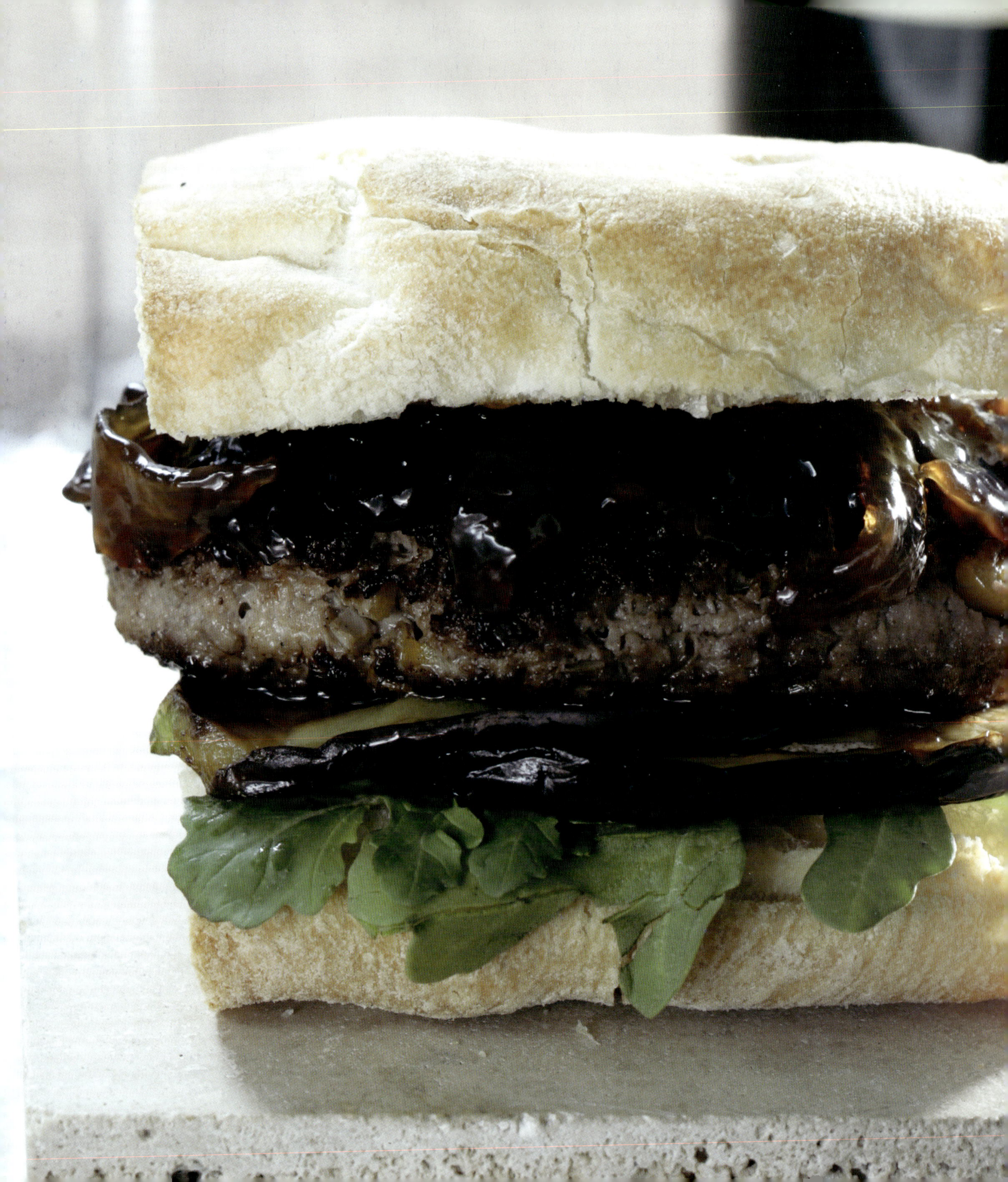

Jumbo Pinotage Lamb Burger

I always wanted to have a burger that could be matched with a great red wine like Pinotage.

Ingredients

3	red peppers, quartered and deseeded
1	large aubergine, cut into 12 slices
40ml	olive oil
10ml	chopped fresh rosemary
1	medium onion, finely chopped
2	large garlic cloves, finely chopped
2	slices white bread
100ml	milk
50ml	pinotage wine
	salt and freshly ground black pepper to taste
1.25kg	minced lamb

Onion Marmelade

2	onions, finely sliced
10ml	olive oil
50ml	pinotage wine
50ml	balsamic vinegar
40g	brown sugar

Serves 6

Method

Turn the griller in your oven to high.

Arrange the peppers skin side up on a baking tray and grill until the skin blackens and blisters.

Remove the pan from under the griller and place peppers in a plastic bag; let them cool in the bag and then peel away the skin.

Meanwhile heat a frying pan on the stove until hot, add the olive oil and fry the aubergines until soft and golden.

Soak the bread in the milk for about 5 minutes.

In a mixing bowl, mix the rosemary, onion, garlic and mince together. Squeeze the bread dry, crumble it and add to the meat mixture. Add the wine, mix well and adjust the seasoning.

Divide the mixture into six portions and form into patties. Fry the patties in the pan for about 4-5 minutes per side.

Place a buttered bun on a plate; place the patty on the bun, top with aubergine, red peppers and onion marmalade. Serve immediately with either a salad or chips.

Onion Marmelade

In a saucepan, heat the oil and fry the onions until golden. Add the pinotage, balsamic vinegar and brown sugar.

Simmer until the mixture starts to thicken.

Serve hot on the pinotage burger.

Notes

In place of the lamb you can use beef mince. A mixture of lamb and ostrich mince is also a good call.

Desmond Tutu

*Archbishop Emeritus and
Nobel Laureate*

Nelson Mandela said it best with his description of the man "in the purple dress", known fondly across South Africa as "The Arch": "Sometimes strident, often tender, never afraid and seldom without humour – Desmond Tutu's voice will always be the voice of the voiceless."

South Africans can be very thankful that this son of a teacher and a domestic worker was raised in an atmosphere of tolerance and empathy.

Tutu says he "never learnt to hate", and it was in exactly this spirit that this small man with a huge personality in the worst of times urged the victims of apartheid not to hate, and to "choose the peaceful way to freedom".

Tutu became a pivotal international voice for the anti-apartheid movement and, inevitably, came under attack as he spoke out boldly against its injustices. He was targeted for harassment and denied a passport to travel abroad, but eventually the South African government withdrew the restriction in the face of mounting national and international pressure.

It was no surprise to anyone when in 1984 Tutu won the Nobel Peace Prize, the second black Nobel Laureate, in recognition of "the courage and heroism shown by black South Africans in their use of peaceful methods in the struggle against apartheid".

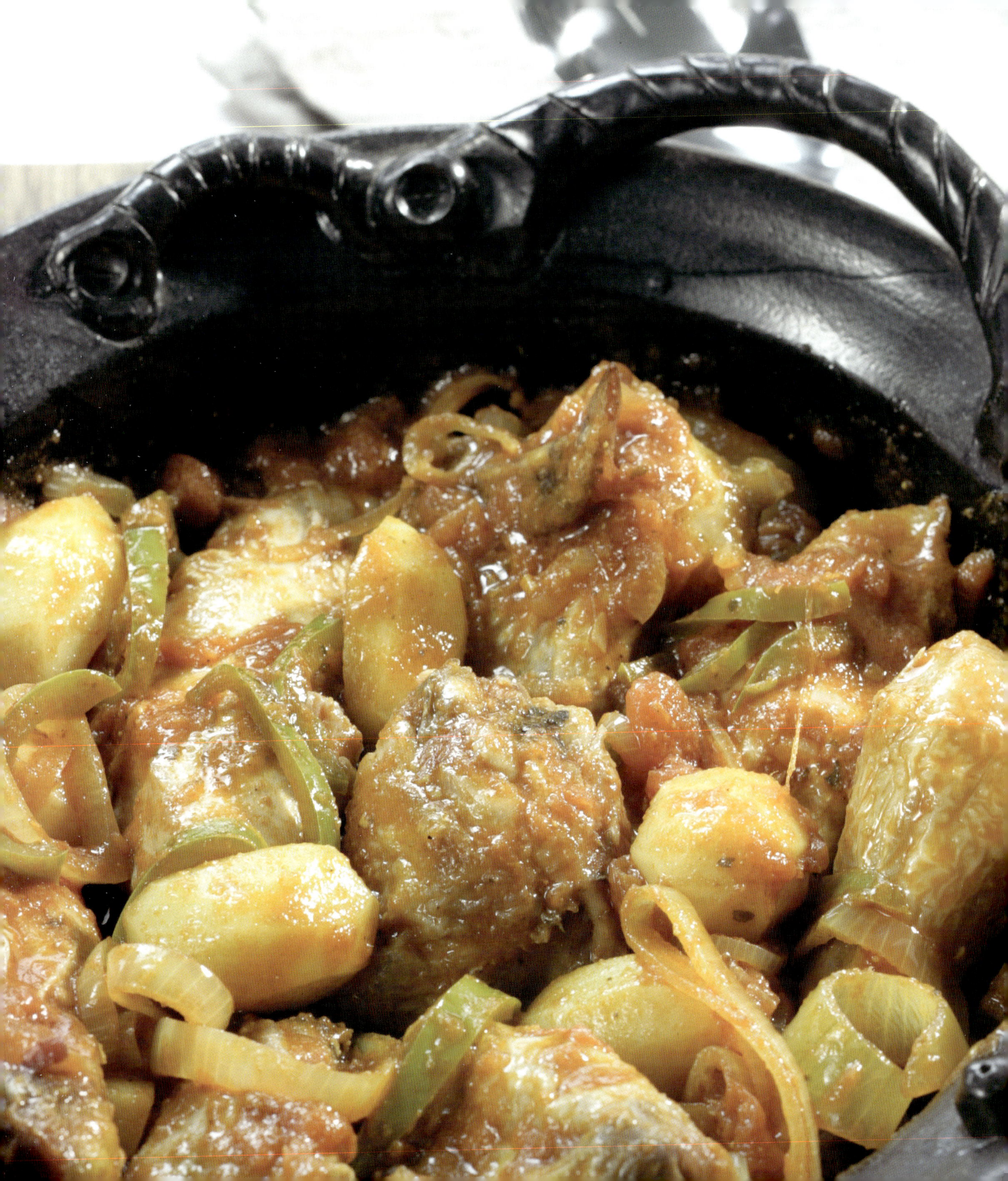

Tutu Chicken

Dishes such as these are ideal for large functions. The chicken can be prepared beforehand; and the potatoes can be boiled ahead of time, and then peeled and sliced just before baking.

Ingredients

3	potatoes
2	large tomatoes, skinned and chopped
1	whole chicken cut into portions
400g	can tomato purée
75g	seasoned flour
15ml	curry paste
45ml	vegetable oil
5ml	tabasco sauce
2	onions chopped
1	chicken stock cube
1	green pepper sliced
600ml	water

Serves 4

Method

Boil the potatoes in a saucepan for ten minutes until half cooked. Remove from the pot, let cool to room temperature then peel and slice.

Coat the chicken in the seasoned flour. In a saucepan, heat the oil and brown the chicken pieces. Remove from pan and place in a casserole dish.

Pour some of the fat off from the saucepan. Add the onions and green pepper and sauté until soft.

Sprinkle the remaining seasoned flour over the vegetables and mix through. Add the tomato purée, curry paste, tabasco sauce, stock and sufficient water to make a thick sauce.

Cover the chicken with the sauce, and arrange the sliced potato on top. Cover the casserole and bake at 150°C for an hour or until the chicken is tender.

Notes

Serve with rice and a salad.

Walter Ilz

The Legend of the Culinary Landscape

The ebullient, larger-than-life Walter Ulz loves being out in the front of his restaurant as much as he enjoys creating exciting dishes. A traditionalist who uses his palette of constancy on which to create exciting cuisine – that's Ulz, chef-patron of the multi-award winning fine dining restaurant, *Linger Longer* in Sandton.

His bulging files of newspaper cuttings celebrate the noteworthy people who have been regular visitors over the years. Celebrities, the "who's who" in politics, business and just about every sphere of the South African landscape, "some even from the Braamfontein days", where *Linger Longer* first started some thirty years ago.

"Although we've broken away completely from the old menu and now do a seasonal thing with exciting new influences, we've retained the traditional *Linger Longer* dishes," says Ulz.

Awards – for the restaurant, the wine list, as well as the chef-patron – have pride of place as you enter the restaurant. And so it should be. Ulz himself is one of the country's "noteworthy people" – loved by all who appreciate a fine palette combined with all-encompassing warmth.

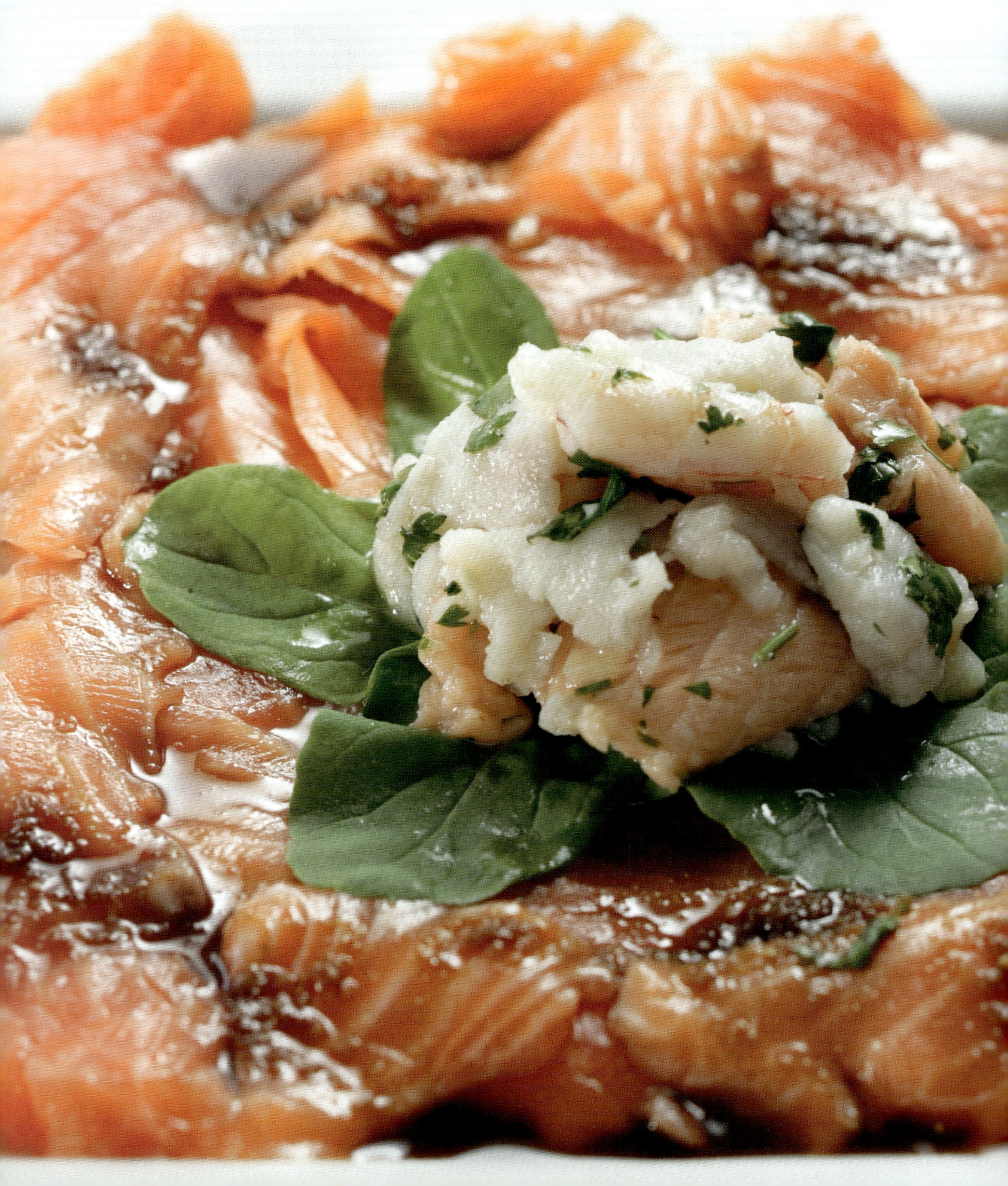

Salmon Carpaccio topped with Seafood Cerviche

The combination of flavours in this dish is a taste of heaven!

Ingredients

200g	fresh salmon, thinly sliced
200g	fresh prawns, shells removed and poached for a few seconds
200g	fresh line fish, sliced (mussel cracker or cod)
	juice of 6 fresh limes
	juice of 6 fresh lemons
10ml	coriander leaves
10ml	honey
5ml	finely chopped garlic
2.5ml	finely chopped chilli
5ml	brown sugar
5ml	pink peppercorns, crushed
	salt and freshly ground black pepper

Salmon Carpaccio

900g	fresh salmon, thinly sliced
	juice of 2 lemons
30ml	fresh ginger, grated
30ml	teriyaki sauce
15ml	wasabi sauce
10ml	coarse salt

Serves 6

Method

In a mixing bowl, mix together the lime and lemon juice, coriander leaves, honey, garlic, chilli, sugar and pink peppercorn.

Add the salmon, prawns and line fish.

Adjust the seasoning and leave to marinate for at least 30 minutes in the refrigerator.

Salmon Carpaccio

Place the thinly sliced salmon in overlapping leaves on a plate. Mix together the lemon, ginger, teriyaki, wasabi and salt, and drizzle over the carpaccio.

Notes

Top the carpaccio with a serving of the cerviche and garnish with rocket leaves.

Mary van Apeldoorn

Recruitment agency owner and Board & Executive Committee Member, Business Against Crime Western Cape

Businesswoman could well be a word created especially for Mary van Apeldoorn, who never believed the world of finance and accounting was the exclusive domain of men.

Twenty years ago she started her one-woman recruitment agency, which is today one of the most respected human resource companies around.

And she's no shrinking violet either in that traditionally male world of big business; Van Apeldoorn's business acumen and experience have seen her honoured as the first woman vice president for the Cape Chamber of Commerce and Industry, since 1804, and the first female president of the Institute of Credit Management SA in 1990. And she counts the following among her achievements too: Van Apeldoorn is a qualified International Personnel Consultant, an Honorary Fellow of the Institute of Credit Management, and a Fellow of the Institute of Directors.

She's definitely the person to ask about how to secure that dream job; she's a specialist in everything from interview preparation to a perfect curriculum vitae. Her client base ranges from blue chip companies to small businesses, and her success, Van Apeldoorn believes, lies in her commitment to high standards, the best candidates and a steady dose of diligence.

Just as she pulled herself up by her own bootstraps, Van Apeldoorn wants the best for the people she employs. "We actively promote personal growth and development," she says.

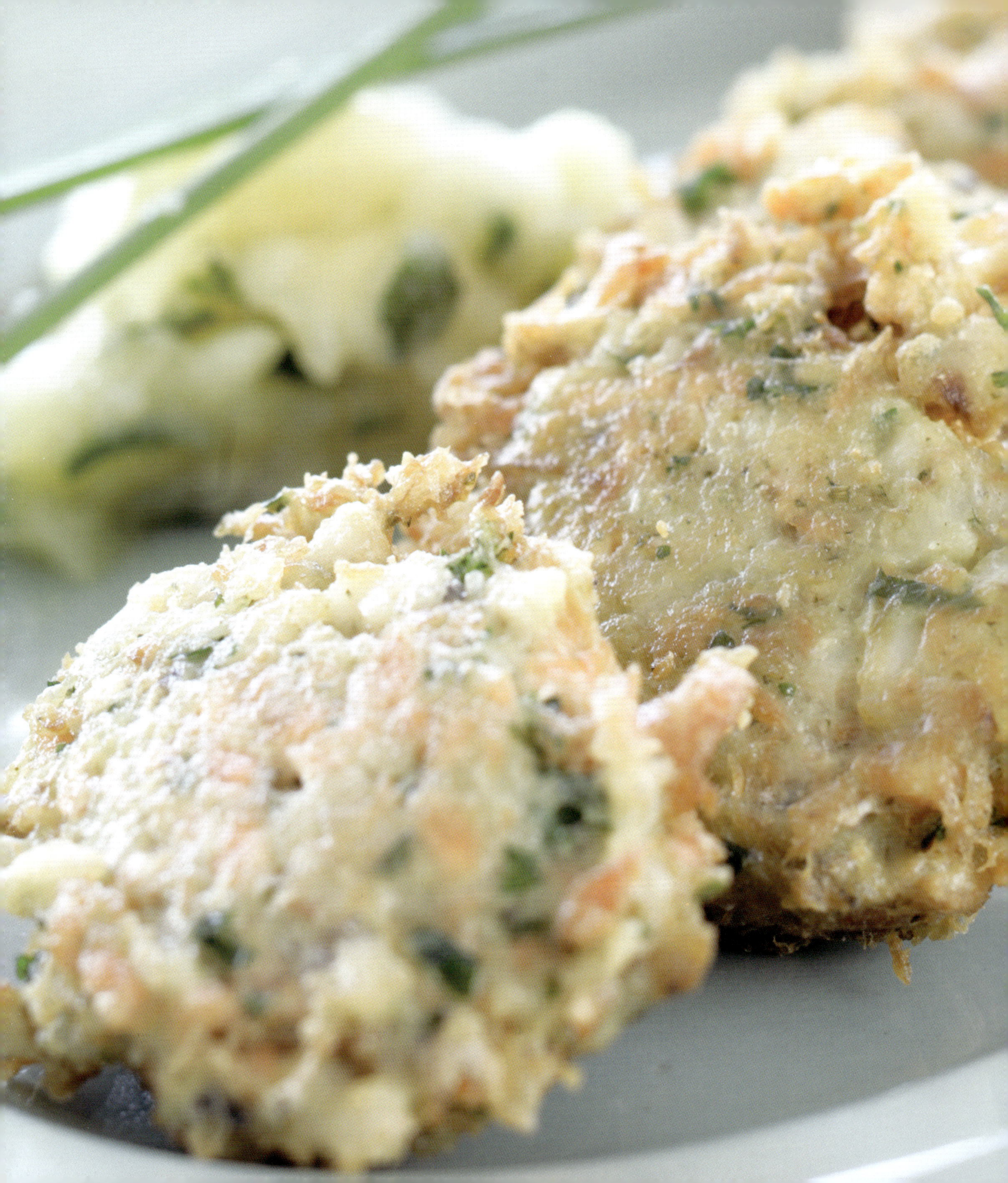

Fish Cakes

Mary van Apeldoorn, makes the best fish cakes ever. I have used this recipe for snacks, light meals and even as a starter with some sweet chilli and lime sauce. I loved the recipe so much I also have it in my book, *Home Cooking*, not the grand version as this one, but it still ended up on the front cover!
Francois Ferreira

Ingredients

1kg	fillets of hake or any firm white fish, cleaned and skinned
1kg	Canadian salmon
3	lemons
30ml	fish spice
5	bay leaves
375ml	white wine
250ml	fish stock or water
3	eggs
60ml	Thai pesto
60g	chopped dhania
60 g	chopped parsley
1	chilli, seeded and chopped (optional)
1	large onion, finely chopped
250ml	tempura flour
500ml	oil

Serves 6 for a main course and about 15 for snacks

Method

Preheat your oven to 180°C.

Place the fish fillets in a rectangular ovenproof dish, squeeze the lemons over the fish and place the squeezed lemons on top of the fish. Sprinkle the fish spice over and add the 5 bay leaves, then pour the wine and water/stock over everything, cover with foil and bake in the oven for 20 minutes or until the fish is soft.

Remove the fish from the liquid and flake, then add the eggs, Thai pesto, dhania, parsley, onion, chilli and tempura flour. Mix all the ingredients together and allow to rest in the refrigerator for 1 hour.

Remove from the refrigerator and fry spoonfuls or formed cakes in oil until golden brown and firm.

Serve with mashed potato and sweet chilli sauce.

Notes

Should you not be able to get Canadian salmon, just double up on the white fish.

Thai pesto is relatively easy to make – use the same process as for basil pesto but use dhania instead and add the flesh of 1 chilli.

Maizina or potato flour can be used instead of tempura flour.

Peter Veldsman

*Renowned Restaurateur,
Food Writer and Gastronome*

This is the man who invented the term "potjiekos", who went on to get his bistro invited to move to the V&A Waterfront, and who believes "the best of the best" is all that's good enough for his patrons.

It's hardly surprising then that this owner of Emily's Restaurant is the first recipient of the Galliova Award as South Africa's best food writer for magazines, member of the Chaine des Rotisseurs – and the author of 10 cookbooks.

Peter Veldsman's restaurant is a South African institution and one of the most acclaimed in the country. But it's also home to the Culinary Art Institute of Africa, founded by Veldsman in 1994 as a hands-on facility to train future chefs, service staff and restaurateurs.

He was food editor of *Sarie* magazine for more than 16 years, but Veldsman's diverse talents have seen him produce several television series and even appear himself on the small screen, alone or with Emily's chef Johan Odendaal.

South African food is his passion, but his restaurant serves up fare from all parts of Africa, with the search for top ingredients leading them off the continent altogether sometimes – they serve only the best Norwegian salmon.

In his Woodstock days, Veldsman's Emily's was described as "the eccentric of the restaurant scene". And latest descriptions of it since its move to the Clock Tower as "more polite", but "still hardly mainstream", only make it more interesting.

Everyone knows the life of a restaurateur means little time off work, but home for Veldsman is "an old Victorian house filled with art and antiques – and four naughty dogs".

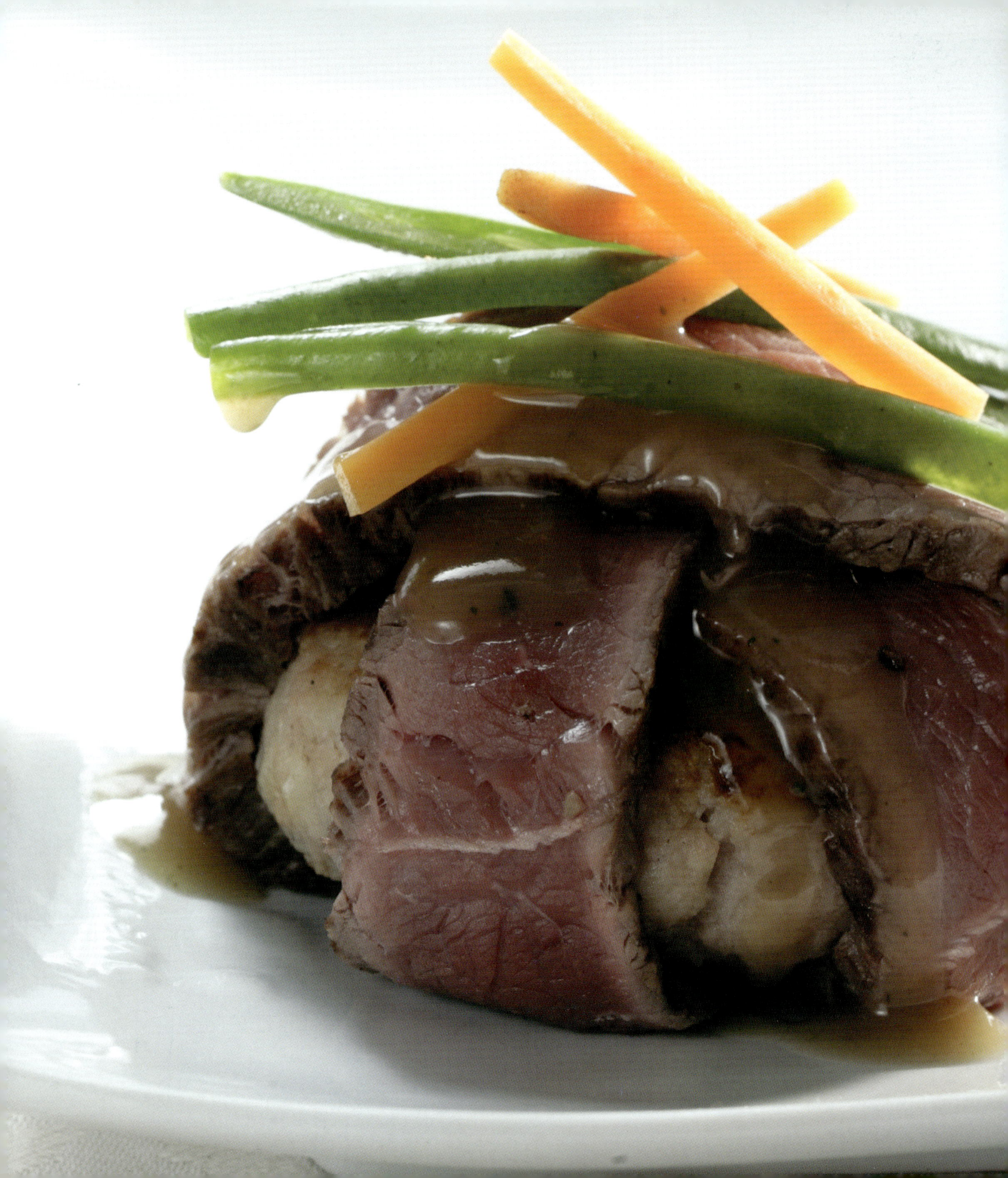

Beef and Pork 'Pie'

Don't get a fright if the recipe looks more daunting than it actually is. It is very different, and your guests will be suitably impressed.

Ingredients

Filling

50ml	coarsely grated carrot
50ml	coarsely grated onion (with juice)
50ml	finely chopped celery
15ml	sesame oil
75ml	olive oil
30ml	finely chopped fresh parsley
10ml	chopped fresh oregano
5ml	chopped fresh rosemary
500g	good quality pork sausages
125ml	dry breadcrumbs
50ml	finely grated dry parmesan cheese
3	extra large eggs, beaten
5ml	freshly ground black pepper
5ml	ground ginger
	salt to taste

Remaining ingredients

10	portions beef sirloin, with a little fat layer (approx. 250g each)
	butter and oil
	salt and freshly ground black pepper

Serves 10

Method

Place the carrot, onion, celery, sesame and olive oil in a mixing bowl and mix well using a two-pronged fork. Add the parsley, oregano and rosemary and mix well.

Cover the bowl with cling film and refrigerate for 30 minutes to allow the flavours to develop.

Remove the sausage meat from the casings and place in a large mixing bowl. Add the breadcrumbs and cheese, work the dry ingredients through the meat using a two-pronged fork (work with care using a cutting rather than mixing action).

Add the eggs, pepper, ginger and raw marinated vegetables. Mix without "kneading". Taste and add some salt, if needed.

Divide the pork mixture into 10 equal parts – shape each part into a meat patty, using a ring or mould with a diameter of 75mm. Place next to each other on a greased baking tray, cover with cling film and refrigerate until needed. Can be prepared 36 hours in advance and kept well refrigerated.

The meat

Place a cast iron griddle pan over medium-high heat and add a little oil to the pan. Heat until smoking hot.

Add a little more oil to the pan as well as a knob of butter. Sear each portion of the meat on both sides. Remove the meat from the griddle and place the portions, each time they are seared, on a wire rack placed over an oven-roasting pan. This last step can be done an hour before needed and just left in a cool place or at room temperature. DO NOT season the meat at all.

To prepare the 'pie'

Preheat the oven to 160°C. Place the oven pan (with the meat on the rack placed over the pan) into the preheated oven and roast 12-15 minutes until medium rare, depending on the thickness of the meat. Remove and place in a preheated warmer drawer for 20-30 minutes – the resting period is of utmost importance.

Meanwhile, place the pork 'patties' in the still heated oven and bake for 8-10 minutes until cooked through.

To assemble

Place a ring mould with a diameter of 100mm on a warmed dinner plate. Remove a portion of the sirloin from the drawer and season well with salt and pepper. Place on a cutting board and slice the meat on a slant into slices of 3-5mm thick.

Arrange the slices on the inside of the mould on the plate, overhanging the sides.

Place a 'pork patty' in the mould and fold the overhanging meat back over the pork filling. Press lightly with the palm of the hand; remove the mould.

The sirloin will resemble the 'pie crust' with the pork forcemeat as the 'filling' for the 'pie'.

Serve with sautéed mushrooms, rich brown gravy and a rocket side salad. You can also top the pie with steamed julienne vegetables.

Topsi Venter

*Acclaimed Restaurateur
and Food Judge*

If Franschhoek is indeed the food and wine capital of South Africa, then acclaimed foodie Topsi Venter is surely one of its first citizens. Owner of the aptly-named Topsi & Company restaurant in the town, Venter's food is universally described by besotted diners in ways that get the mouth watering.

Some plain old praise for this legend of Cape culinary circles is that there is "always a taste of South Africa in everything she produces". Honoured with the Eat Out Johnny Walker Lifetime Award in 2004, the multi-faceted doyenne of South African foodies has at different times been described as a chef extraordinaire, eccentric, lovable and a loyal friend, and a storyteller supreme.

In 2003, she launched her limited edition recipe book – which was actually more of an artwork – *Fooding Around With Topsi*. Illustrated by artworks commissioned from 26 of Cape Town's top artists, it features her signature recipes. Venter says her food is eclectic, not something that can be boxed, but she does admit to a basis of French cooking with a penchant for Malaysian spices.

Ever down-to-earth, one of Venter's favourite quotes is from the legendary James Beard, recognised by many as the father of American gastronomy: "It is a small miracle to be a good cook. When you grow old, even ugly, people will still find the path to your door."

You can bet food lovers will long be finding the path to Venter's door.

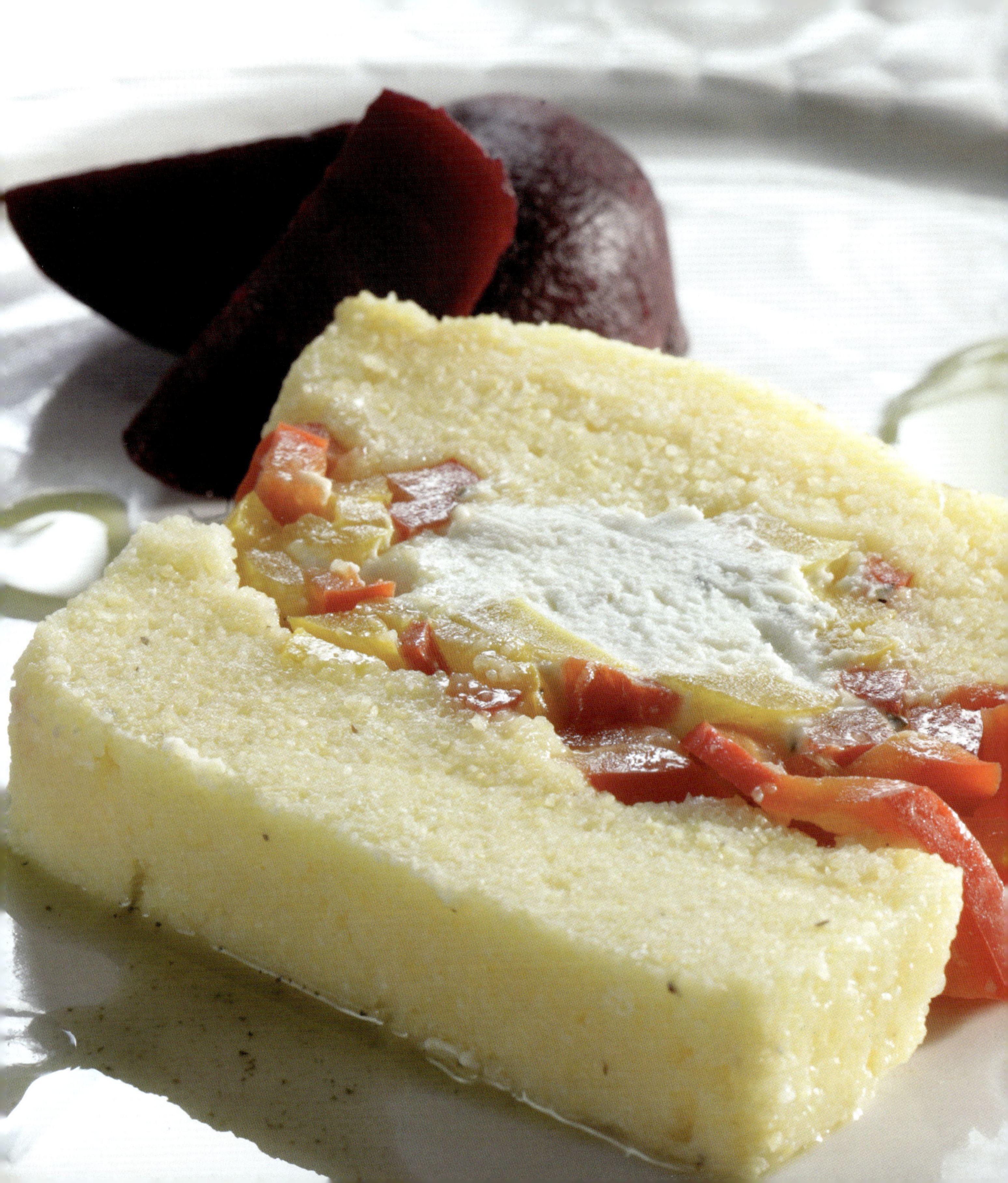

Polenta Terrine with Chevre and Pickled Red and Yellow Peppers

This recipe is from my book *Fooding about with Topsi*. It is ideal as a starter for a spring luncheon or as part of a vegetarian meal. The glowing yellows and deep reds of this dish, accentuated by the white sparkle of the chevre will delight your friends – vegetarians and carnivores alike.

Ingredients

150g	instant polenta
625ml	vegetable stock
12.5ml	salt
2	cloves crushed garlic
25g	butter
5ml	coarse black pepper
2	chevre goat's milk cheese logs (2x120g)
250g	pickled red and yellow pepper
	beetroot wedges, spring onions, olive oil to garnish

Serves 4

Method

Bring the 625ml of stock and the salt to the boil, in a heavy-based saucepan.

Whisking continuously, add polenta in a thin stream until the mixture returns to the boil.

Add garlic cloves, black pepper and the butter.

Using a wooden spoon, stir polenta over low heat for 4-5 minutes until very thick.

Line a bread tin with greaseproof paper or cling wrap. Pour in a thin layer of polenta. Lay half of the pickled peppers over the first layer of polenta.

Now place the cheese logs down the centre and cover with the polenta. Use up your last pickled peppers and cover with remaining polenta.

Refrigerate until set. Remove from bread tin one hour before needed.

Notes

Slice with a hot knife and place carefully on a warmed plate. Serve with oven-roasted beetroot wedges, chopped fresh spring onions, and drizzle with olive oil.

Martin Welz

Editor Noseweek

Rushing in where angels fear to tread is a quality on which this award-winning investigative reporter and founder editor of *Noseweek* definitely prides himself. Welz's motto for his unique publication is after all "all the news you are not supposed to know". This motto – as well as legal threats involving vast amounts – is second nature to this famous newshound in his pursuit of the truth.

The attorney turned journalist, who has spent most of his working life challenging everyone from top politicians to big business, had a dream to earn a living from selling news, rather than what those paying for their advertising believed should be printed.

Since *Noseweek* was founded in 1993, unlike mainstream publications in South Africa and abroad, Welz has scorned advertising revenue in favour of "uninhibited reporting of the facts", a decision that may not have made him rich, but which certainly has won him national and international acclaim.

Irreverent is a word often used to describe him, along with others as diverse as the not-so-kind "a near legend" *(Mail & Guardian)*, and "a national treasure" (former *Sunday Times* editor Ken Owen), which Welz, calls "too kind".

There are those who, afraid of the facts, prefer to regard his work as "wild satirical invention", but the fact that Welz has been threatened with legal action many times, but has rarely been sued – and never successfully – tells the story like it really is.

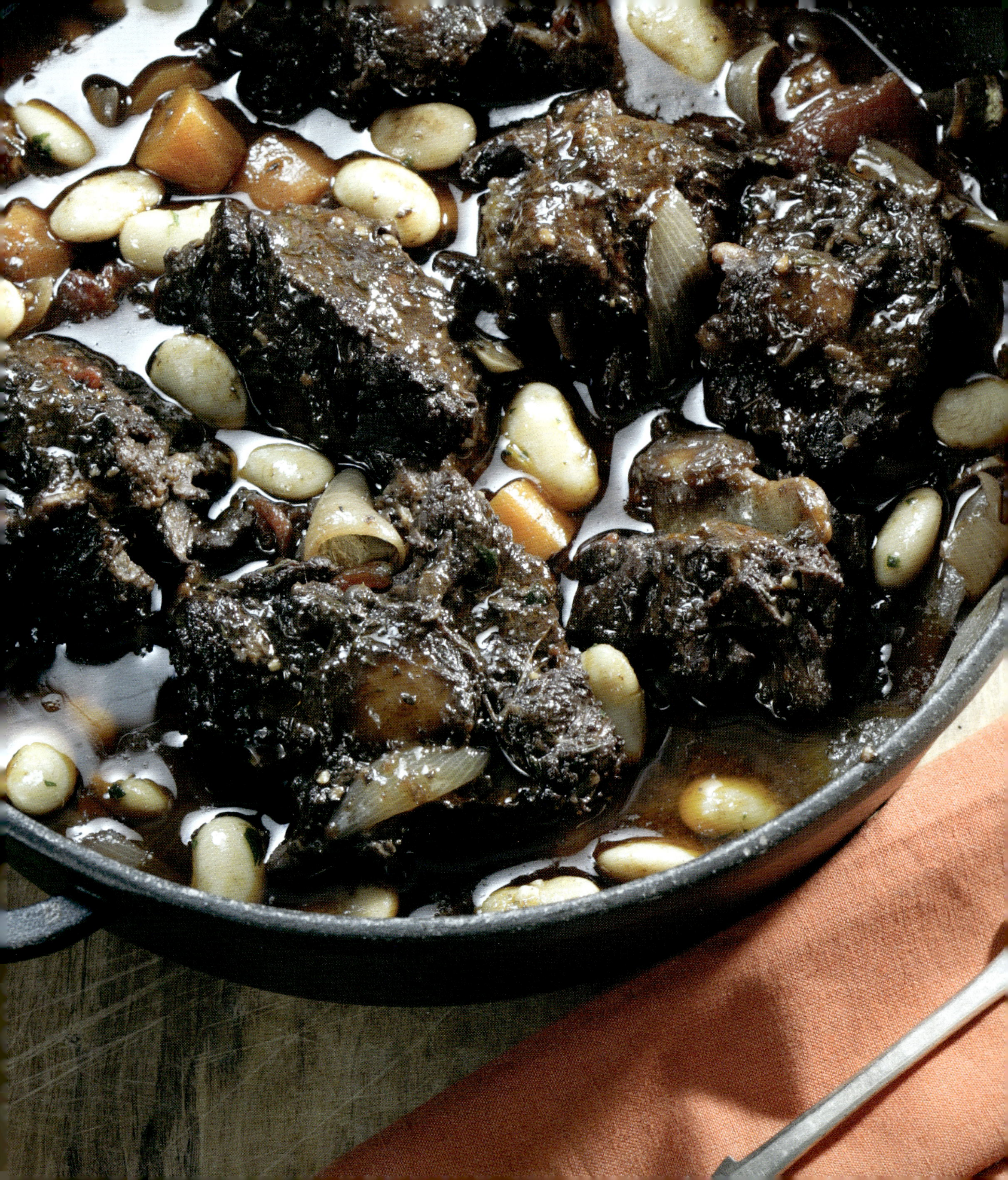

Slow-cooked Oxtail and Beans

My working days are spent investigating and exposing crime and corruption. Having fought the good fight for a week, the weekend is for cooking a meal to share the joys of good food and good company. This dish always does it for me.

Ingredients

1.5kg	thickly sliced oxtail
15ml	olive oil
1	large onion, finely chopped
4	carrots, sliced
1	clove garlic, sliced
1	tin tomatoes in juice, crushed (410g)
1	tin butter beans, drained (410g)
	a handful of fresh thyme
	a handful of celery leaves
1	bay leaf
750ml	chicken broth or beef stock
250ml	dry red wine
	salt and freshly ground black pepper
	more thyme for garnishing
	crusty bread

Serves 4

Method

Trim the excess fat from the meat.

Place all the ingredients in an oiled, heavy casserole, just large enough to accommodate it all nicely, and enough stock to cover. Don't add the salt yet, in case it toughens the beans.

Cover with 2 sheets of oiled greaseproof paper and a tight-fitting lid. Bake at 100°C for 8-10 hours or until meltingly tender.

Remove meat and keep warm. Skim off the fat and reduce the cooking liquids over a high heat to a suitable consistency.

Check the seasoning and garnish with fresh thyme.

Serve with delicious crusty bread and a glass of shiraz.

Notes

Slow cooking will allow the flavours to blend and develop into the most delicious meal you've had in a long time.

Kango Wines (Pty) Ltd
PO Box 46
Oudtshoorn
6620

Tel: 044 272 6065
Fax: 044 279 1038
Website: www.kangowines.com

Van Rensburgs Foods
60 Courtenay Street
George
6529

Tel: 046 874 4746
Email: vrfoods@mweb.co.za

Anlo Guest House
C/o Guthrie & Eiland Streets
De Kelders
Southern Cape

Tel: 028 384 1201 (Ezette Meyer)
Tel: 083 457 8711
www.anloguesthouse.co.za
Email: anlo@kingsley.co.za